MW01222298

Declutter Your Mind:

How to Free Your Thoughts from Worry, Anxiety & Stress using Mindfulness Techniques for Better Mental Clarity and to Simplify Your Life

Marie S. Davenport

© Copyright 2018 by Marie S. Davenport - All rights reserved.

The contents of this book may not be reproduced, duplicated or transmitted without direct written permission from the author.

Under no circumstances will any legal responsibility or blame be held against the publisher for any reparation, damages, or monetary loss due to the information herein, either directly or indirectly.

Legal Notice:

This book is copyright protected. This is only for personal use. You cannot amend, distribute, sell, use, quote or paraphrase any part or the content within this book without the consent of the author.

Disclaimer Notice:

Please note the information contained

within this document is for educational and entertainment purposes only. Every attempt has been made to provide accurate, up to date and reliable complete information. No warranties of any kind are expressed or implied. Readers acknowledge that the author is not engaging in the rendering of legal, financial, medical or professional advice. The content of this book has been derived from various sources. Please consult a licensed professional before attempting any techniques outlined in this book. By reading this document, the reader agrees that under no circumstances are is the author responsible for any losses, direct or indirect, which are incurred as a result of the use of information contained within this document, including, but not limited to, —errors, omissions, or inaccuracies.

Table of Contents

Introduction

Chapter 1: Getting Started to Decluttering Your Mind

Chapter 2: Shifting Your Mindset: From Cluttered Negative Thinking to Clutter-Free Mental Clarity

Chapter 3: Why your Mind is Filled with Clutter - And How to Fix It

Chapter 4: Effective Meditation - Being in the Present Moment

Chapter 5: Organizing Life Priorities: What Matters the Most

Chapter 6: Managing Daily Tasks for Better Productivity and to Avoid Getting Overwhelmed

Chapter 7: How to Achieve Work-Life Balance

Chapter 8: Remaining in the Moment at

Work

Chapter 9: Home Management 101:
How to Effectively Declutter Your Home

Chapter 10: Choosing a 'Less is More'
Lifestyle for Worry-Free and Stress-Free
Living

Chapter 11: Taking it to the Next Level
with a Tiny House

 Bonus Chapter: Getting Rid of Digital
Clutter to Maximize Technology Use and
Simplifying Your Life

Conclusion

DECLUTTER YOUR MIND

PEACE

FOCUS

BALANCE

CLARITY

Introduction

Congratulations on owning *Declutter Your Mind* and thank you for doing so. Making the decision to clear out your mental clutter once and for all can be a difficult one and for that, so give yourself some credit.

Unfortunately, there is often far more to it than that as mental clutter is an often insidious threat that can be difficult to pin down, even if you are looking for it. To help you reach your goal successfully, the following chapters will discuss everything you need to know about clearing your mind of excess clutter as quickly and easily as possible.

Inside you will learn everything you need to know about mental clutter, how it forms and what you can do to get rid of it. You will find a variety of tasks and exercises designed to do just that, as well as a few designed to help you take things a bit farther still by doing things like decluttering your physical space and considering minimalism in all its forms. You will even find a bonus chapter that discusses the perils of digital clutter and what you can do to stop it from forming once and for all.

There are plenty of books on this subject on the market, thanks again for choosing this one! Every effort was made to ensure it is full of as much useful information as possible, please enjoy!

Chapter 1: Getting Started to Decluttering Your Mind

Chapter 1: Getting Started to Decluttering Your Mind

1.1 Understanding Mental Clutter

It is easy to see the way clutter builds up in the real world, slowly but surely it can take over a shelf, a room, maybe even a whole home. Mental clutter is much the same, sticking in the corners of the mind and slowly building until it is difficult to get a single thought in edgewise that isn't part of the existing paths your mind has built to deal with the detritus.

In order to move forward with the process of decluttering your mind, you are going to need to clean out all of your mental clutter and start fresh. What's more, dealing with mental clutter isn't something you will only have to do once after you have cleaned your mental house, you are going to need to learn to remain ever vigilant to ensure that it doesn't start building once more.

Mental clutter is the stuff that keeps us stuck in self-sabotage, suffering, struggle, stress, and separation. It is the stuff that makes life hard and complicated. It is the stuff that puts us at odds with everyone else.

Hidden where eyes can't see, mental clutter lurks wherever peace and love don't. As long as we're cluttered, we're resisting the flow and ease of life.

If you are not experiencing clarity, peace, and love, you have mental clutter. It lives exclusively and elusively in your thoughts. It starts as a head-fog, cloudy and misleading, and evolves into something much bigger.

Clutter composes the stories we tell about ourselves that cripple our potential and attack our well-being. It says we can't, we shouldn't and we won't. It gives cause for doubt and mistrust, leaving us feeling helpless   in   the   world.

1.2 **Benefits of removing mental clutter**

Removing the mental clutter that is blocking up your mind is essentially like removing individual layers from an onion. In this scenario, if you want to get at the truth of the way the world looks around you, and you haven't cleaned out your mental clutter in a while, then that truth is covered in various layers of misinformation, beliefs (accurate and inaccurate) related thoughts and stories you tell yourself. Luckily, as long as you take the time to clear out your mind from time to time, the effects of mental clutter aren't permanent.

If you have ever spent a prolonged period of time feeling more deeply connected to the universe and the people around you, then the good news is that you can feel that same sense of unity, love, and peace at all times, that was a moment when all of your mental clutter was cleared and you were free to operate at maximum efficiency.

Unfortunately, most people are far more focused on the state of their bodies than they are their minds. This focus on eating right and staying fit is compounded by the desire to work as much as possible, which in turn can make it difficult to find the time to exercise and eat right. This issue is then compounded by the needs of others that they want to help meet, their own needs that need to be met in order to keep the whole process moving and a million other little things fight for their time.

This frequently means the mind gets the short end of the stick, but this can be far more detrimental than you might expect. The fact of the matter is that every other aspect of your life, from relationships to your career, to your body all hinge on the health of your mind. Thus, if you don't find the time to nurture your mind and clear out the mental clutter then everything else is sure to suffer sooner or later.

When it comes to decluttering your mind, the ultimate goal is always going to be clarity and a sense of peace that can't be manufactured in any other way. You will feel a return to a state of almost innocence where you are free from any drama, dogma or stigma that you might be holding onto. While you might feel as though these are the things that prop you up at first, with time you will see all they are really doing is holding you down.

1.3 Looking for symptoms of mental clutter

One of the most nefarious parts of mental clutter is the fact that many of its aspects serve to mask the fact that there is an issue in the first place. As such, if you have let your mental clutter build up unchecked for years, then you may be extremely cluttered without even realizing it. If you are worried this is the case, consider the following list of symptoms and see if they apply to you.

1. *Confusion:* Do you find yourself frequently confused by things that you used to handle with ease? A sense of general confusion, often accompanied by either fear, worry, or both; as well as a general sense of feeling scatterbrained are all signs you may be dealing with an influx of mental clutter.

2. *Chatty inner voice:* Everyone has a mental narrator who operates in the back of their mind to some degree. If that voice seems to never shut up, then you may be dealing with an influx of mental clutter. If your inner dialogue goes from normal amounts to what amounts to a constant noise in the background, then this should be

considered a red flag of potential mental clutter.

3. *Chaos:* While there are always going to be certain events in our lives that sow disorganization, and chaos when they appear, this should be the exception, not the rule. As such, if you find that you are always dealing with a large amount of chaos in your life, either physical or mental, then you may need to take a closer look at your mental clutter and see if that isn't part, or all, of the problem.

4. *Conditions:* When it comes to mental clutter, having an influx of conditions can also be thought of as having lots of requirements,

stipulations or prerequisites on your daily routine or the activities and events you take part in most frequently. If lately, you have been feeling as though everywhere you turn there are limits, rules, and boundaries, either external or internal, then you may be dealing with an influx of mental clutter.

5. *Collections:* If you are someone who has always been drawn to the idea of having the complete set of something, then taking an analytical approach to your desire to collect may be difficult. Unfortunately, this can be a clear sign of increasing mental clutter which means it is important to find a way to measure your collections that makes sense for

you. If left unchecked, mental clutter can increase one's desire to stockpile physical representations of past success as a means of increasing feelings of security and comfort. After all, the cluttered mind reasons, if I'm feeling extra anxious keeping these things around will make me feel better. A good indicator that your desire to collect has gotten stronger is if you have recently begun to expand an existing collection or if you have just started an entirely new collection.

6. *Comparisons:* If you generally tend to classify yourself as a happy person, but recently find yourself looking at those around you and feeling as though the things you

have don't really stand up, then mental clutter could well be to blame. This sort of desire is often generated as a result of an unfulfilled desire to seek out better and more interesting activities or challenges, often those that are just over the next hill. If you find yourself comparing yourself to those around you more regularly than before, mental clutter may well be to blame.

7. *Worry:* This is one of the most potentially dangerous types of mental clutter of them all. What makes worry so insidious is that it can make not just the time before a specific event occurs unbearable, it can also limit your

full potential and make any negative outcome you were stressing out about much more likely to actually come true. Worry will also make it far easier for you to look at the world in absolutes as opposed to more realistic shades of gray.

8. *Guilt:* Guilt is a difficult type of mental clutter to excise as once you have given into it you can easily become trapped in a scenario where your worst mistakes are played back to you endless while you are left wondering what you could have done differently. If not handled properly this can lead you to a cycle where the only real outcome is despair and it becomes

increasingly difficult to even consider trying anything new. While guilt in certain situations is perfectly understandable, if not exactly healthy, you will be able to tell if your guilt is the result of mental clutter if you find yourself retaining deep feelings of guilt for relatively minor issues.

9. *Negative self-talk:* Self-criticism can be beneficial if restricted to a healthy measure. However, there is a limit to the amount of negative conditioning you can subject your mind to before it starts becoming counter-productive. There is a sea of difference between, "I really need to be more physically active" and "I am a lazy blob." Excessive self-loathing can heavily backfire

because it shifts the focus from ways through which we can improve to our failures. Over a longer period, thrash negative self-speak can up your stress level, and lead to major depression. Learning to tame negative self-talk is the key to overcoming challenges, feeling more confident and achieving the life of your dreams.

10. Negative self-talk is another type of mental clutter than can be difficult to pinpoint, especially if it has been building for quite some time. The key, then, is to keep a list of the types of things you find yourself saying to yourself throughout the day. While these negative quips might fly under the

radar at the moment when you look back on them after the fact the pattern should be far more pronounced.

Long-term effects: If left untreated in the long-term, mental clutter can potentially throw you completely out of sync with your thoughts, leading to a feeling as though there is an overall lack of harmony in the world at large. In fact, the feeling of mental fog that you feel can ultimately evolve into a crippling form of malaise that has the potential to last for weeks, months or even years. In so doing it has the potential to cripple your potential in all aspect of your life, making it difficult to believe or trust anyone, even those closest to you. You will also lose faith in your abilities and find it difficult to deal with the world at large. This is why it is vital that if you find any mental clutter you do what you need to do in order to eradicate it posthaste.

Step ①

Your Quick Start Action Step: Create a baseline

The first step towards finding mental clutter is to take stock of the current state of your mind. This can be something that you write down, or it can be something you track mentally, what matters is that you take a flashlight to all the various corners and little used rooms in your mind and take stock of what you find there. Look in all the places you would expect to find mental clutter and see what you find.

Not only will doing so provide you with a roadmap of things that you will need to focus on in the near future, but it will also provide you with a baseline that you can measure yourself against in the future. This way you will be able to track how much progress you have made, sort of like a before and after photo that some people take while working out. Regardless of your preferred method of analysis, you should keep some concrete record so that you have something to look back on during moments of self-doubt or when it seems as though you aren't making progress so you can see how far it is you have really come.

Chapter 2: Shifting Your Mindset: From Cluttered Negative Thinking to Clutter-Free Mental Clarity

Chapter 2: Shifting Your Mindset: From Cluttered Negative Thinking to Clutter-Free Mental Clarity

2.1 Fixed and Growth Mindset

As children, some people are told they excel in certain subjects while others are told that they succeeded because they tried hard and that effort leads to success. The first group of children can be expected to develop a fixed mindset whereby their brains become more active when they are being told how well they have done. The second group of children can be said to have a growth mindset wherein their minds are the most active when they are learning what they could do better next time. Those with a fixed mindset tend to worry more about how they are seen by others than what they are actually learning which is why those with a growth mindset tend to be more successful in the long run.

Fixed Mindset

- Wants to look smart or competent regardless of the reality
- Quick to avoid challenges
- Easily thwarted by obstacles
- Thinks effort is "pointless"
- Ignores feedback
- Can feel threatened by the success of others

Growth Mindset

- More interested in long-term results.

- Enjoys a challenge.
- Learns from obstacles
- Equates effort with success
- Appreciates criticism
- Finds inspiration in the success of others

The two mindsets also manifest themselves differently when it comes to dealing with setbacks. When those who have a fixed mindset are met with a setback it directly affects how they see themselves because it shakes their belief in their innate talent. This makes it easier for them to give up on something they are struggling with as they can easily tell themselves that it is just not a talent that is in their wheelhouse. On the other hand, when a person with a growth mindset is met with a challenge they instead worry about the best way to overcome it and treat the issue as an opportunity to learn and grow.

By this point, it shouldn't be hard to see which of the two mindsets is going to be more prone to acquiring mental clutter, and also which is likely required in order to clean out your mind once and for all. A fixed mindset is particularly dangerous in this scenario as it can balk at the work ahead in hopes of finding an easy workaround. This is something that you simply can't abide, however, and if you hope to clear your mind you are going to need to make a conscious decision to focus on this situation with a growth mindset and never look back.

2.2 **Change for the better**

With the consequences of having a fixed mindset so potentially disastrous, especially if you are striving to find the inner strength to clean out your mental clutter once and for all, it is important to do what you can to break these negative mental habits as quickly as possible. Luckily the human brain has the ability to constantly reshape itself throughout the course of its lifetime which means that it is never too late to shift into a growth mindset, no matter how deeply rooted the fixed mindset principles might be. New neural pathways in the brain can be formed as new thoughts are repeated time and again, and once they become well-worn paths, then new habits are formed.

When it comes to creating new neural pathways, one of the best ways to do so is by seeing a noticeable result from an action that you consciously took in an effort to change your mindset, such as the exercises described below that will help you experience a mind that is clutter-free. While a single positive choice or two a day won't generate noticeable results on their own, their cumulative effect can be substantial and that typing point can occur sooner than you might think.

While you are getting used to keeping up a growth mindset on the regular, you may find that remaining positive and feeling empowered is easy as long as everything is going well, only to have things fall apart as soon as the struggle is added to the equation. Those who originally had a fixed mindset are going to have a much more difficult time powering through times of adversity at first, but if they ever hope to find a way to truly empower themselves then they will need to remain positive and see it through as that is the only way that new neural pathways are ever going to be successfully formed.

When working to keep a growth mindset in all things, it is important to keep it up even when the going gets tough. It will likely seem like the easiest thing in the world to do while things are going well, but a fixed mindset is much more likely to manifest itself during times when roadblocks begin presenting themselves. Your fixed mindset will likely make you want to abandon all hope of forward progress when these road blocks appear.

In this case, it is important to make an effort to stop thinking of the challenges as roadblocks and start thinking of them as opportunities for you to learn and grow. Finding personal ways to meet the challenges that come your way head on without dwelling on them unnecessarily is the first step towards making a real change for the better. If you are having difficulty putting this idea into practice, consider the following:

- Take the time to look for the silver lining and consider what opportunities that meeting this challenge head on will give you access to. Dealing with problems as soon as they arise will typically provide you with the opportunity to handle the issue in a simpler fashion or take actions to stop the situation from otherwise getting out of hand. Learning to appreciate this opportunity will make adopting a growth mindset much easier.

- Use the challenge in question as a mirror to reflect challenges you might be having when looking to improve other facets of your life. If everything is going smoothly then it can be easy to overlook important information that could come back to bite you later if left untreated for too long. Dealing with challenges directly can, in turn, then provide you with insight into what else in your life deserves a closer examination.

- Consider the possible reasons behind why you feel the way you do. When you are face to face with roadblocks you will often find that they are easier to approach if you have a growth mindset as it will allow you to take that extra moment to stop and really consider whatever it is that you are going through. A quick run through of the facts will often reveal the fact that roadblocks will be easier to overcome than they might have at first. This is often thanks to a personal bias that you were harboring that you likely didn't even know was affecting you. If your deeper analysis reveals that the road block is more mental than physical, you need to be comfortable in your growth mindset to let the mental block go.

2.3 Experience a Clutter-Free Mindset

The exercises in this section have all been chosen to help you start to get used to the type of clear, clutter-free mindset you should be fostering. You won't need to worry about forcing a clear mindset in these scenarios, all you need to do is focus on the task in question and the desired mindset should manifest itself. Once you get used to this new and improved mindset, you will then be ready to start actively working towards it more regularly.

1. *Brain writing:* Take a piece of paper and, as quickly as you can,

write down any issues that come to mind. Keep writing until you have nothing more to add. Next, take a look at your list and acknowledge that you will deal with these concerns at an appropriate time.

With this out of the way, you will find that you are now free to devote yourself fully to the task that you originally wanted to focus on. Ideally, you will want to take a journal and fill at least three pages each morning. Hand written is important in this case, not in digital form. The kinesthetic aspect of writing in longhand form is a key to its effectiveness.

The content of your morning pages can be anything that's on your mind. Even if the thoughts you're writing are negative, putting them on paper is cathartic for the mind; this simple technique helps to clear out your mental cobwebs so you can devote yourself more fully to the creative tasks each day holds. It's like taking a dust-buster and poking it around into the corners of your mind. By transmuting these thoughts into physical form, on paper, you can set them aside – both literally and figuratively – and enter your day more refreshed and creative.

The same technique works equally well in group brainstorming sessions. Plan for some "warm up" time to get participants into a creative frame of mind, just as you would stretch prior to exercising. Solicit the group's top of mind thoughts and ideas but – here's the important part – don't stop there. The first ideas that brainstorming participants throw out are typically the obvious solutions, and they tend to be of fairly low value. Keep pushing the group farther outside of their comfort zone via a variety of playful activities and ideation exercises. This is where some of the greatest insights and highest-value ideas will likely emerge.

2. *Play Music:* Playing music is a popular creative outlet. While any

type of music is equally effective, if you aren't serious or talented with an instrument, it should serve you even better as a mental decluttering exercise because you have no objective to improve. Your only goal is to play.

If you already play an instrument, you know what to do: just spend some time with it and zone everything else out. Make this a session in clearing your mind, rather than in getting good at a song or writing something new that others would enjoy. In other words, don't try to perfect your Canon in D, but rather play something you already know and don't have to think about, or just mess around with simple scales and progressions.

If you don't already play an instrument, pick up one of these instruments that require little to no knowledge to begin messing around:

- Hand drum or Djembe
- Gong
- Singing Bowl
- Chime
- Kalimba
- Maracas
- Your voice (There's a reason why singing in the shower is so fun — it feels good.)

A popular instrument that requires zero talent is the

Kalimba, an African instrument typically made out of a coconut shell and 5-8 metal keys. It becomes meditative and there is no way you can make a mistake. Ukuleles are also fun instruments to pick up even if you have no experience with music. They only have four strings, and the strings tend to be softer since they're nylon, and so easier on your fingers. Learn a couple of strumming patterns and a few chords and you'll be well on your way to enjoying the mini string instrument.

Remember, the purpose isn't to wow an audience — it's to focus your attention on creating rhythm, melody, and sound.

3. *Go for a Hike:* Nature and exercise are both prescriptions for improved health and well-being. Henry David Thoreau made a good point when he said, "I took a walk in the woods and came out taller than the trees." It's because nature feels good. It nourishes the body, mind, and spirit. Combine them and what you get is time well spent. Countless poems have been written and studies have been published about the benefits of nature and the sheer awe and magic that it can offer.

Find a hike near you. Try searching AllTrails.com to find a new route. As you hike, bring awareness to your breath as you move. Notice the sensations in your body, observe how your heart rate increases on the hills, and watch your calves engage as you descend. Notice every detail of your surroundings, the colors, the plants and fauna, any animals you pass, the rhythm and pace of your movements, and your feet as they hit the ground in a cyclical manner. Take it all in without distraction.

4. *Watch a Sunset:* A great way to instill yourself with a present feeling is by watching the sun say goodbye for the day. Aside from its natural beauty, the sunset is also a brilliant reminder that each and every day offers us a new end and a new beginning. Get lost in the

vibrant colors and spirit of the sunset and take Mother Nature's advice that the rest of your to-do list can wait until morning.

5. *Work in the Garden:* While it would be easy to blast music while you plant your petunias, try to cultivate a quiet, mindful state of being as you work in the garden. If you can keep the music off and your mind focused on paying attention to what you're doing in the garden — the sensations of your hands in the dirt, the breeze across your face, the smell of the incoming basil, and your breath as you move, you can turn your gardening session into a mindfulness practice.

6. *Dance:* Put on some trance or ambient music without words, close your eyes, and allow your body to move freely. Try using an open space like the yard, living room, or basement, and dance like no one's watching because, well, no one's watching. And it feels good.

7. *Bake:* Baking requires focus. You have to follow the directions precisely, otherwise, you could end up with a hard, burnt, inedible object when your family is eagerly awaiting banana bread. Choose a recipe that you've never tried before and one you may consider complicated, make sure your ingredients are out on the kitchen table, (and make sure you have

them ALL, otherwise your exercise in mindful baking could quickly turn frazzled,) and begin.

As you follow the steps, pay attention to your breath and the task at-hand. When you mix the batter, turn the spoon or whisk slowly and mindfully, taking in the smells and changes in texture along the way. As you spread the batter into the pan, take extra care in making sure it's even and smooth. When your treat is ready, follow the steps at the end of this post to eat mindfully, enjoying every morsel of your masterpiece.

8. *Write a Note:* Choose someone in your life you appreciate and write them a handwritten note. Perhaps

it's to thank them for something they did, the type of person they are, or maybe it's for no reason at all except to tell them the things you admire about them.

Before you begin writing, close your eyes and picture an image of this person in the center of your mind. Take a few breaths. Notice what feelings come up when you have this person at the center of your mind.

Now jot down a list of 5-10 things about this person — adjectives that highlight their talents, words that describe how they make you feel or how they've helped you, or anything else that would make them feel good.

Now write them a note using your list as fuel. If you want to get extra fancy, you can include a small gift of gratitude and hand deliver it. Otherwise, you can send it in the mail. Cultivating awareness and gratitude can be helpful tools in supporting your mindfulness practice. Plus, it will doubtlessly make the day of this special person in your life.

Your Quick Start Action Step: Pay Closer Attention

With the proliferation of screens across all forms of technology, people are increasingly being rewarded for dividing their time among as many different tasks as possible. As a result, there is far less time to focus on the smaller details of a given situation and consider the types of meaning that are only found upon closer consideration. Therefore, the first step in becoming more perceptive is going to be taking note, not of what you are missing, but of the fact that you are missing it.

To get started down this path, all you need to do is stop for a few moments once or twice a day to consider what is going on around you and think about how much you are currently missing out on throughout the day. The specifics here don't matter, as long as you slow down and take the time to look at life from another angle. This could include something adventurous like hiking a new trail every weekend, or it could be something simple like making a point of noticing what your coworkers are wearing each day, the specifics don't matter as long as you work on it each day and start building a new skill in the process.

Chapter 3:
Why your Mind
is Filled with
Clutter - And
How to Fix It

Chapter 3: Why your Mind is Filled with Clutter - And How to Fix It

3.1 Your brain on clutter

Described as anything that is kept, even though not used, needed or wanted, clutter can also be defined as having a disorganized and overwhelming amount of possessions in our living space, cars or storage areas. But clutter isn't just physical. When you have to-do items constantly floating around in your head, or you hear a ring every few minutes from your phone, your brain doesn't get a chance to fully enter creative flow or process experiences. Clutter creates stress that has three major biological and neurological effects on us—our cortisol levels, our creativity and ability to focus, and our experience of pain.

The overconsumption of digital stuff—like social media notifications, news feeds, games and files on our computer—competes for our attention, creating a digital form of clutter that has the same effect on our brain as physical clutter. Neatness and order support health—and oppose chaos.

So, what is going on? Our brains love order. The human body consists of thousands of integrated and interdependent biological and neurochemical systems, all organized and operating along circadian rhythms, without which our bodies would disintegrate into chaos. It's no wonder that the organization within our very own bodies naturally extends to the desire for order and tidiness in our homes. And order feels good, in part, because it's easier for our brains to deal with and not have to work so hard.

3.2 The science of cortisol

No matter the ways, reasons, and means by which the creep of stuff exceeds our ability to mentally and physically manage it—all of it amounts to stress. Clutter can trigger the release of the stress hormone cortisol, which can increase tension and anxiety and lead to unhealthy habits. Cortisol is a hormone produced in response to stress by the hypothalamus-pituitary-adrenal axis (HPA).

Chronic clutter can create prolonged stress, throwing us into a state of low-grade, perpetual fight-or-flight—the system designed to help us survive. The fight-or-flight response involves the complex interaction of many body systems and organs that activate needed functions and minimize unnecessary functions during times of stress. These systems must remain in balance to maintain optimum physical and psychological health.

According to a Cornell University study from 2016, stress triggered by clutter may also trigger coping and avoidance strategies, like eating junk food, oversleeping or binge-watching Netflix.

If we are not stressed, we get most of our cortisol in the morning to get us going. Levels taper off the rest of the day if we are relaxed, enabling us to enjoy psychological and physical wellbeing. But a messy home environment can prevent our body's cortisol levels from naturally declining throughout the day. Taxing this system eventually results in higher levels of depression and anxiety, and a lower capacity to think clearly, make decisions, and stay focused.

To supply the body with the energy needed to deal with stress, there are several physiological changes that occur with elevated cortisol levels:

- Diversion of blood flow to the muscles from other parts of the body
- Increased blood pressure
- Increased heart rate
- Increased blood sugars
- Increased fats in in the blood

If there is no relief from stress, all of these changes are bad for healthy brain activity and can cause lasting negative changes in brain function and structure. Additionally, when stress raises the body's cortisol levels, its overall health can be adversely affected, including organ damage, the suppression of the immune, endocrine and reproductive systems, the lowering of the metabolism, and the disruption of the sleep cycle, to name a few.

It is difficult to maintain a state of wellness over time when the body's energy is channeled into coping with stress.

Just as concerning, when the body is in a state of chronic stress and not thinking clearly, the brain tends to only see that which is negative as these are, historically, the things that could turn into threats. Unfortunately, all this does is reinforce the pre-existing sour point of view, perceived lack of social support and subsequent poor interrelationships.

Research from a 2009 study out of UCLA's Center on Everyday Lives of Families (CELF) has shown that women who perceive their homes to be cluttered tend to have unhealthy patterns of cortisol levels. A team of professional archaeologists, anthropologists, and other social scientists studied the home life of 32 middle-class, dual-income families with 2-3 children of ages 7-12 in Los Angeles. In the study, family members recorded self-directed home tours describing objects and spaces in their homes, during which saliva samples were taken at regular intervals to measure cortisol levels.

The data were collected for three days and compared to and correlated with vast amounts of other data previously collected over the course of four years. According to the CEFL study, the amount of stress women experience at home is directly proportional to the amount of stuff they and their family had accumulated.

It's interesting to note in the UCLA study that men did not exhibit the same results, having normal cortisol fluctuations. Presumably, they were not as stressed by the amount of stuff in their home. This can be explained possibly by the results of other studies that have shown that the home is traditionally perceived as women's domain and ultimate responsibility, even in households where both partners work.

Other studies also support the finding that if men don't think the responsibility of keeping the house tidy is relevant to them, they may not be inclined to see the clutter and so are not as stressed about it.

This may be explained further in part by research that has indicated that there are distinct differences in vision between men and women since men have 25 percent more neurons in their visual cortex, a part of the cerebral cortex that processes visual information. The irony is that even though the visual cortex of a man has more neurons than a woman's, men are impacted more by the things they see that they think have to do with them, and less by the things they think do not.

The brain has a limited capacity to process information. To filter out extra stimuli and focus on what we are trying to achieve at any given moment, the top-down and bottom-up attention mechanisms compete. By mutually suppressing each other, brain power is exhausted, and ultimately we lose focus. Whether we know it or not, a kitchen counter stacked with mail and basket full of unfolded laundry can be as distracting to us as a toddler in the throes of a tantrum.

3.3 **Start to declutter**

Now that we know what all of our extra stuff is doing to our health and ability to function, it's time to get rid of it, right?... Oh, but if it were only that easy. Although most people don't experience heightened ACC/Insula activity to this degree, we can all identify with the feeling of angst when finally tossing that pile of unread magazines, or those ticket stubs from last summer's trip to New York to see Hamilton. The good news is, those who suffer from hoarding respond well to Cognitive Behavioral Therapy. For the rest of us... there is decluttering.

In addition to improving your mood and focus, decluttering often acts as a catalyst for taking better care of other aspects of our life. By purging unneeded items from our homes, it is like deleting files to create disk space on your computer. Suddenly, the whole operating system is more efficient...this decreases stress and increases your effectiveness personally and professionally.

While actually going ahead and getting rid of unnecessary items will be covered in detail in a later chapter, the exercises in this chapter are going to cover the preparation you will need to do in order to get ready to declutter once and for all. This lifestyle change requires two things: a vision list, and a why list. You will want to start with your vision list. This list is going to be everything you want to accomplish from your future results. Your list can, and should, contain anything that is important to you and serves as a reason for why you are making this lifestyle change. The more unique and personal this list is, the better it will serve you.

If you are having a hard time getting started, here are some things you might consider writing on your vision list:

- I want to eat healthier at every single meal
- I want to experience the loving relationships in my life, every day
- I want to contribute to the world in a meaningful way, daily
- I want to read and write on a daily basis

- I want to be passionate about every single day that I'm alive
- I want to take risks in life
- I want to be present in every single moment

These visions are essentially what you want to accomplish through your minimalist lifestyle. After you are clear on what you want to achieve with your new lifestyle, you want to get clear on why. Understanding why you want change is what will compel you to actually make the change. So, after you completely your list that outlines everything you want, you can start a list right beneath it that is going to tell you every reason why you want it. You should make sure that both lists are as detailed as possible. If you have several important items on your vision list, and on your why list, that is completely okay. You should not feel as though you have to limit yourself. The more reasons you can provide, the easier the entire transition is going to be for you.

As you become more aware of what you want, as well as why you want it you should find that it becomes easier and easier to motivate yourself to actually start working towards achieving your dreams. While you may feel as though your good intentions are strong enough to get you through right now, not listening to your mental clutter can be more difficult at the moment than you might expect. That is why it is important to have your vision and your why. These are lists you will refer back to when you are feeling internal resistances. You can regroup, refocus, and start all over again in a new frame of mind that will allow you to have an easier ability to achieve your desired results.

Your Quick Start Action Step: Start working on your vision list

As discussed above, your vision list is the linchpin that holds your motivation together. You don't need to put it together all at once, however, if you need some time to work on it that is perfectly fine. You can keep a running tally of things to add to it whenever you think of a new one. This process doesn't have to stop either, you can add something new to your vision list whenever the need strikes you.

Chapter 4: Effective Meditation - Being in the Present Moment

Chapter 4: Effective Meditation - Being in the Present Moment

4.1 **An ancient practice**

Mindfulness meditation is a type of meditation which focuses on being as aware of each moment as possible, thereby helping the consciousness to expand by forming a stronger connection with the present. Mindfulness meditation has a long history of practice as part of the Buddhist faith where it is revered for its ability to improve both mental happiness and physical well-being. This has been corroborated by research which shows that mindfulness meditation is a beneficial treatment for a variety of mental conditions. What's more, it has also been shown to be effective when treating conditions including anxiety, stress and drug addiction.

While mindfulness can be practiced almost anywhere at nearly any time, the concept began as a structured meditation technique practiced by Buddhists known as vipassana. Roughly translated this means to live in the moment while understanding that sometimes you must be aware of the future as well. The general idea is that achieving vipassana will allow you to come to understand the universe as a whole and comes through the knowing of a few key principals.

The idea of practicing mindfulness first caught on in the Western world in the early part of the 1970s. Professor Jon Kabat-Zinn is credited with creating a mindfulness based method of stress reduction which paired mindfulness with yoga to great result. While Zinn didn't do anything particularly new, the fact that his techniques led to measurable improvements for a wide variety of ailments both mental and physical in turn led to additional studies on the topic. These studies have shown time and again how effective practicing mindfulness can be which in turn has led to a steady increase in the practice to the point where it can now be found being regularly practiced in schools, veteran treatment facilities, hospitals, even prisons.

4.2 Many benefits

In addition to helping improve self-discipline, studies show that that taking 15 minutes out of your day to practice mindfulness meditation has a host of additional benefits as well. For starters, it is known to show dramatic increases when it comes to projecting a strong sense of self while at the same time noticeably reducing stress. This is thanks to the positive effects that mindfulness meditation has on attention span, emotional regulation and body awareness. What's even more impressive, neuroimaging has shown that mindfulness meditation actually allows those who practice it to process information more quickly than those who do not.

The activity can also literally improve the health of the brain as studies show that those who started practicing mindfulness meditation at a young age actually have more volume in their brains as they age.

Meditating regularly is also known to increase the thickness of the hippocampus which means that it actually makes it easier to learn new information and retain it for a prolonged period of time. It also positively affects the amygdala which means those who meditate are less likely to experience stress, anxiety, and fear. With so much going on under the hood, is it any wonder that those who meditate tend to report an overall increase in mood, temperament, and wellbeing?

Beyond these noticeable physical changes, regularly practicing mindfulness is known to help improve self-discipline in additional ways by decreasing instances of meditators' minds getting stuck in negative thought patterns while also making it easier to focus for prolonged periods of time. A recent Johns Hopkins University study found that practicing mindfulness meditation regularly is equally effective at treating anxiety, depression, and ADHD as many commonly prescribed drugs.

Other reasons to practice mindfulness meditation

- Mindfulness meditation naturally leads to a deeper understanding of the self and allows many people to take stock of their strengths and weaknesses, leading to personal growth.

- Studies show that those who practice mindfulness regularly have a stronger memory, leading to an easier retention of facts in both the long and the short term.

- In addition to the specifics, mindfulness meditation improves overall physical wellbeing with those who practice regularly reporting fewer instances of illness and a more rapid recovery when they do fall ill.

- Mindfulness meditation can help improve emotional control while at the same time increasing one's threshold for pain.

- As surprising as it might seem, making a habit of being mindful can actually make even the most middling music seem more engaging. This deeper level of engagement leads to a general increase of enjoyment, regardless of the type of music or any previous musical preferences.

- With a regular dose of mindfulness meditation, many people experience a dramatic increase in their ability to empathize with others no matter what the situation. Furthermore, it allows practitioners to listen to other viewpoints more actively, more compassionately and results in their ability to withhold judgement on thoughts and ideas that differ from their own.

4.3

While practicing mindfulness meditation might seem like a tall order at first, the truth of the matter is that being mindful is a habit which means you can learn to improve through practice, practice, practice. In fact, it should be one of the easier habits in this book to get accustomed to as it is as easy as taking a few moments out of your day to focus exclusively on the present via all of the information that your senses are bringing in.

1. *Getting started:* When you first start practicing mindfulness, it is important to always practice at the same day to ensure your body is going to get into the habit of entering a mindful state each and every day, to make the transition easier to manage. Don't forget, it takes about a month for a new habit to solidify in your mind which means that as long as you can keep it up for that amount of

time you can keep it up indefinitely.

In order to reach a state of mindfulness, you are going to want to find someplace comfortable, and quiet to sit, though not so quiet and comfortable that you are tempted to fall asleep. Then, all you need to do is breathe deeply, in and out. As you breathe in, focus all of your attention on the information that your senses are providing to you, focus on the way the air feels in your lungs, how it smells and how it tastes. Slowly but surely, expand your consciousness so that you are taking in as much information about your surroundings as possible.

2. *Observe the moment:* Mindfulness is not necessarily quieting the mind or finding an eternal state of calmness. The goal here is simple. We want to pay attention to the moment we are in without judging. When we judge a thought or something we may have done in the past, we tend to dwell on it. That isn't living in the moment and is not conducive to mindful meditation. While this is easier said than done, it is a crucial step to mindful meditation. With practice, it will be easy to achieve. Be mindful of the moment, of your senses and your surroundings.

3. *Ignore those pesky judgments:* Take notice of the times you are

passing judgment while practicing. Make note of them and move on.

4. *Always come back to observation and the present moment:* It is easy for our minds to get lost in thought. Mindfulness meditation is the art of bringing yourself back to the moment, over and over, as many times as it takes. Don't get discouraged. In the beginning, you will find your mind wanders a lot. Reel it back in and keep moving forward.

5. *Be kind to yourself:* Even if your mind does happen to wander, and it will, don't be hard on yourself. It happens. Acknowledge whatever

thoughts pop up, put them to the side and get back on track.

Practice mindfulness at all times

Once you get the hang of the basics of mindfulness meditation you will find that there is practically nothing you can't do that doesn't lend itself to being mindful. The following are some of the easiest ways to get into the habit of practicing mindfulness meditation around your home, but you can also practice at work, on public transportation, or even while driving. With a little extra practice, the wide variety of times you can easily slip into a mindful state are sure to surprise you.

Interact with social media mindfully: While it may seem surprising if you go about doing so in the right way, spending time with Facebook or Instagram can actually be a very mindful experience. While it is easy to get distracted from your goal while interacting with social media, with practice you will find that the time you spend doing so can leave you feeling quite centered and ready to face the next challenge that awaits you.

In order for this type of mindfulness to be effective, the first thing you are going to want to do is to limit potential distractions as much as you can. This is crucial due to the fact that most people interact with social media while multitasking which will make practicing mindfulness much more difficult. Once you have cleared the distractions out of the way you will then want to clear your mind and focus on the moment as much as possible. After you have found the correct mindset, you will then want to revisit old pictures from activities you were a part of and try your hardest to relive those events as thoroughly as possible.

With each picture you see, do your best to try and remember everything you were doing at the moment. Think back to the way you felt and really let the experience wash over you. Throw yourself back into the moment with all your might and remember the various signals your mind was bombarding you with at the time. After you have returned to the memory, take the time to think about how the space that you are once again occupying smelled, as well as the physical sensations. Remember the way the temperature felt on your skin, the sounds of the memory and the things your ears were focused on whether you were actively aware of them or not. With enough practice, you will realize that you have the ability to block out virtually all of the stimuli in the present day and exist solely in your memories.

Your Quick Start Action Step: Start the day off right

It doesn't matter what drink you use to start off your day, be it coffee, tea or something else, you can use that time to practice mindfulness which can, in turn, start any day off on the right foot. If you do it properly you can use the sensations, you experience with your morning cup to pull you into the moment with more clarity than most other activities. This may be the only peaceful moment you are going to get in the entire day, make it count.

1. Start the morning with your first mindfulness session in mind. Focus on the thoughts you have as you begin to wake up and take note of them without expressly interacting with them. Continue this mindset for as long as possible, stopping before you begin to make your morning beverage.

2. While making the drink, focus on the anticipation of the act, consider the feel of your hands as you prepare the beverage and the other sensations that the act of creation provides.

3. Find a good spot to sit quietly for a moment and focus of the drink. Consider the way the cup feels in

your hands, the smell of the drink and the way it looks.

4. Now slowly take your fist sip, consider the taste of the drink, the way the liquid feels as it moves across your tongue and down towards your stomach.

5. As you drink consider how the beverage makes you feel, consider what benefits it is providing your body to ensure you are able to meet the challenges of the day head on.

6. Pay special focus to only these thoughts as you consume your beverage. If you find your mind wandering, gently bring it back to the task at hand.

7. After you are done, take an extra moment to hold the cup in your

hands and be as present at the moment as possible.

Chapter 5: Organizing Life Priorities: What Matters the Most

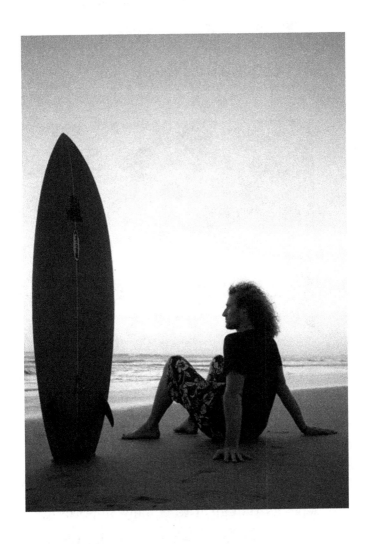

Chapter 5: Organizing Life Priorities: What Matters the Most

5.1 Deciding what is important

Everyone has had that sinking feeling where they realize that they have too much on their plate but are unable to do anything about it. After all, if every task feels as though it is equally important, how do you know where to begin. While it can be easy to feel overwhelmed if you find yourself in this situation, it is important to understand that it is one that everyone has found themselves in at one time or another and, more importantly, it is certainly not impossible to juggle a variety of seemingly competing responsibilities or priorities, it only feels that way at the moment.

The biggest issue in these instances is determining what is actually important and what only feels that way. After all, even if everything feels equally important at the moment you will still need to determine where to start. The most effective means of doing so is through the use of the triple constraint which is a triangle with each side representing one aspect of the task you are contemplating. One side represents the costs of the task, one represents the scope of the task and one represents the time required to complete the task and none can be adjusted without affecting the other two.

As an example, if you were planning to pain your guest bedroom before you have guests next month, then you wouldn't be able to change the scope of the task which is to paint the room, but you could adjust how much time you want the job to take and how much the task might cost because you could hire painters to do the task for you.

5.2 **Be proactive**

While it can be easy to want to plan out your priorities when you feel as though you are getting in over your head, it is far more productive to do so on a regular basis precisely so you can keep yourself from feeling unduly overwhelmed. After all, if you feel as though the walls are already closing in then you are going to have limited options when it comes to improving your situation. If you take the time to deal with the issue when the high-pressure period is still a ways off then you are more likely to come up with an easy solution to avoid it all together. Regardless of when you decide to go ahead and establish your priorities, it is important to stick with the habit and never look back regardless if you are using them at work, at home, or throughout your everyday life. After you really understand the things you need to work on, as well as how long they take, you will be able to make smarter decisions when it comes to whether or not you can take on a new task in the first place.

5.3 **Check your priorities**

In order to ensure that your priorities are currently where they need to be you are going to want to evaluate them individually using the following process.

Make a list: The first step in this process is going to be thinking back through the past three months with the goal of making a list of everything you want to improve, everything you want to change completely and everything you want to work to maintain as is. When looking at your life you are going to want to break your list down into categories, or pillars, that all support your primary goal at the moment. Common pillars include work, health and fitness, personal relationships, finance, and personal life though your pillars should reflect your personal situation.

This initial list is not going to represent your list of goals per se, this list is more freeform than that, instead what you are working on here is the list of core needs that your goals will strive to solve. For example, one of your cores could be to lower your stress level. You could then come up with a goal that would help you to do so in a reliable way. Using your cores as guidelines for the goals you set will allow you to ensure that your goals have a purpose which will, in turn, make it easier to ensure you see them through.

Organize your list: Once you have a general idea of some goals, you will want to ensure that your list of things that you want to improve, change and maintain is being represented in full across your pillars. If there are any extra goals not being covered, consider putting them on the backburner for the moment until you free up some more mental space. After all, there is only so much you can realistically deal with at one time. If you try and do too much at once you run the risk of not actually succeeding at anything.

Add more specifics: Once you have a general idea of your goals and the pillars that they work to support, the next step is to make them as specific as possible which starts by considering which can be completed most easily as well those that will generate the greatest overall benefit in return for the work that you will be putting in. If you are working towards a goal that you are confident you will succeed in then you will want to start with those that will generate the most benefit in the long-term. However, if you are working on a goal that is somewhat out of your wheelhouse you will want to start with the easiest goal as this will help build your confidence and make it easier for you to tackle more complicated tasks.

Judge your goals as a whole: Once you have a general outline for the goals you plan on tackling in the relatively near future, the next step is going to be looking at them as a whole and deciding if they reflect not only who you want to be but also who you are. Put another way, it is important to ensure they hit on all your pillars in a way that can be completed without moving heaven and earth.

Choose where to begin: While it can be easy to get caught up in the planning stage, especially if you are dealing with multiple goals at once, it is important to not use the planning as an excuse to never actually get started. Eventually, you need to be confident in the plans you have made and actually put the rubber to the road. After all, your priorities will never be fulfilled if you don't actively start working towards your goals.

Your Quick Start Action Step: Make your goals SMART goals

SMART goals are specific: Good goals are specific which means you should be able to concisely express them in just a few sentences. They should provide you with a clear idea of the requirements for reaching your goals along with any constraints that may prevent you from reaching them successfully.

SMART goals are measurable: When the goals you choose are measurable it will be clear to you how you will be able to tell if your goal has either been a resounding success or an absolute failure.

SMART goals are attainable: A good goal is one that is realistically attainable which means that you understand any potential roadblocks that may stand between you and the goal in question and that they will be ultimately surmountable.

SMART goals are realistic: A good goal is one that is realistic in addition to being attainable which means that you can expect success without something extremely unlikely being required to push reality into your favor.

SMART goals are timely: A good goal is one that as a clear timetable for when it is going to be completed. Even the best-intentioned goals are likely to fall apart if their timetable is to strict, but also if it is too generous.

Chapter 6: Managing Daily Tasks for Better Productivity and to Avoid Getting Overwhelmed

Chapter 6: Managing Daily Tasks for Better Productivity and to Avoid Getting Overwhelmed

6.1 Discipline is key

While those who are currently in the midst of a bout of depression, lethargy, angst, or whatever other state their mental clutter has left them in, might find it hard to believe, those who are empowered are prone to feeling these things as well. The biggest difference then is that those who are empowered have the self-discipline to not let those feelings get in the way of whatever it is they need to do. While teaching your mind to have a growth mindset is a great first step, improving your self-discipline [2nd step] will make it easier to be more productive and to avoid feeling overwhelmed regardless of how much mental clutter you are currently dealing with.

Being as productive as possible means taking the time to completely understand the intricacies of whatever the task you are currently undertaking turns out to be. The simple fact of the matter is that if you are aware of all of the potential issues the given task might face, you will be able to deal with them much more appropriately when they do manifest themselves. When it comes to empowerment, this means that you are going to want to dig deep on yourself and determine what is truly holding you back so that you can to work on correcting the source of the issues hampering your empowerment, not just its symptoms.

Being truly self-disciplined means knowing when it is best to wait and gather strength and resources and when it is best to strike for optimal efficacy. It doesn't matter how much fact-finding you have done if you never go ahead and pull the trigger. Having self-discipline means acting to work on the issues that are hampering your quest for empowerment, even if they are difficult to face directly. Having self-discipline is a skill which means that the only way it is every going to get easier is with practice. You need to have the dedication to your overall improvement to power through, with the understanding that making the s self-disciplined choice will get easier each time you choose to make it.

6.2 Be ready for what's next

Those who are truly self-disciplined, are that way because they have put in the time required training themselves rigorously to do so. The commitment they have shown isn't something that just appeared overnight, it was the sum of months if not years of dedication to the idea of self-improvement based around the idea that self-discipline is a trait worth fighting to achieve.

On the other hand, at the end of the day, those who have shown commitment and dedication to bettering themselves in the name of self-discipline, get to know the deep, pure satisfaction of being proud of their hard work. The road ahead may be long but the results will certainly be worth it. If you preserve you will be able to stand among the greats and know that you are truly ready for whatever life choses to throw at you next and that you have the self-discipline required to succeed at any and every task yet to fall before you.

When you start actively working to improve your overall level of self-discipline, be aware that it will be one of the most difficult challenges you have ever faced. If you have never actively cultivated self-discipline before then your mind will be trained to prioritize instant gratification which means that it will be set to fight you tooth and nail for what it perceives as your own good. Your own mind will be your greatest enemy but if you persevere you can reach the ultimate goal at the end of the rainbow.

Eventually, however, with enough hard work you will develop the confidence in yourself that is required in order to practice self-discipline all of the time, whenever it may be required. If you master your own mind, there is nothing you can't accomplish keep this in mind and use that perseverance to achieve your goals.

6.3 Check your schedule

1. *Make a schedule:* When it comes to making a schedule, the first thing you will need to do is find the type of calendar or planner that is right for you. It can be a physical item or an application on your phone, the specifics of it don't matter as long as they work

for you in such a way that you are sure to use them consistently. Whatever you choose, it is important to keep all of your scheduling to a single application or day planner as opposed to splitting activities into their own calendars, the goal is to integrate fully, not segregate information and make it more difficult to access and remember.

2. *Analyze your schedule:* With your entire month spread out in front of you, this is a good time to take a long hard look at how you truly spend your time. Use this as an opportunity to trim the fat as needed, but also to expand on areas that you feel are important but are currently neglected. This is

the point where you can most easily make changes that you feel the need to, don't be afraid to put thought into action, the only one that can improve the ways you spend your time is you.

When it comes to prioritizing tasks, it really is as simple as making a list with pros and cons for each of the potential uses for the time in question. You can't be everywhere at once, no matter how hard you try; what's more, no one expects you to be. Be self-confident enough to let others know when you have no more time for additional commitments and you will feel a lot better in the long run. This is the point where you have to make decisions about your time, don't put them off any longer.

During times when you have a large number of tasks to complete in a very specific amount of time, you can then use a similar set of criteria to determine the most effective order to complete them in. When considering the most efficient means of doing so it is vital that you take into account several factors beforehand. For starters, if a specific task looks to be quite tedious but is still more or less straightforward, you will still want to get it out of the way first as it will give you a mental boost and make anything that comes next seem less cumbersome by comparison. However, if one task is significantly more difficult than the rest you may want to set it aside for later so that you can give it your undivided attention when you do decide to tackle it.

3. *Allot timeframes:* Once you know the right order for the tasks you are going to complete, you will want to spend some time thinking about how much time in your schedule you want to devote to each. While scheduling all of your tasks directly back to back might seem like a natural choice at first, it is likely to come back to haunt you as soon as one activity takes slightly longer than normal and all of your other tasks end up behind as a result. Scheduling can be your enemy but it can also be your ally

if you let it. As a general rule of thumb, you are going to want to plan out the time you need for each activity, plus travel time, plus 10 minutes because you never know when something isn't going to go according to plan. After all, the worst that can happen is that you end up 10 minutes early for your next meeting.

Your Quick Start Action Step: Clear your schedule of distractions

If you always feel as though you are running just a little bit late, then it may be because you have too many distractions competing for your time. Before you go ahead and plan out your schedule as described above, make sure to remove any unnecessary distractions first to ensure you aren't budgeting time to account for them without realizing it. The first thing you will want to do is to take a look at your day to day schedule and see what, if any, distractions are common amongst more than one activity. If this ends up being a person or activity that you end up spending lots of scheduled, but also unscheduled, time with then you might need to make dramatic changes, at least until you develop new and improved habits.

Assuming this person or thing takes up a good portion of your time without producing much if any, obvious benefit then there are a few questions you will want to ask yourself. First, consider if the distraction provides you with a means of blowing off steam and relaxing which is not otherwise included in your schedule.

If this is the case then what you see as a distraction is actually performing a vital function by providing you with some relief that the rest of your schedule is lacking. If this is not the case then you will instead need to consider if that time might be better used in another way.

Chapter 7:
How to Achieve
Work-Life
Balance

Chapter 7: How to Achieve Work-Life Balance

7.1 Finding a balance

With technology connecting employers to employees (and freelance workers) after working hours, it's become increasingly tough for people to establish a legitimately healthy work-life balance. You certainly have the right not to tackle work during your personal time, but the fear of losing your job or contracts can add pressure to making yourself available around the clock.

According to a Harvard Business School survey, 94 percent of workers admit to working more than 50 hours a week, and nearly half worked 65-hour weeks. The stress from increased hours and staying plugged into work after hours not only affects your health but can also damage your relationships and overall happiness.

By following a few simple guidelines, it's possible to start shifting the weight toward greater work-life balance.

7.2 Why you need to pull your plug

The technological revolution has made it increasingly easier for people to connect with each other around the world, which has opened the doors for more telecommuting positions within companies. However, just because you can be online all the time does not mean you should be, especially for home-based workers who don't have as obvious a separation in their work-life balance.

Stanford business professors found that workplace stress adds $125 to $190 billion per year to America's health costs. Overworking alone accounts for $48 billion of that total. Ironically, the brunt of health care costs are then covered by the employers who have often established systems that are the source of the stress. In this situation, not only do the employers suffer financially, but there are also other negative consequences on the business due to the decreased productivity of overstressed employees.

Because these costs often seem hidden, they are not properly factored into employers' cost-benefit analysis.

Within the European Union, the costs of overstressed employees are being taken seriously. Some large European companies have now taken steps toward reducing burnout and creating a better work-life balance.

In 2012, Volkswagen blocked emails to employees after-hours, while Daimler moved to delete emails of employees on vacation. After the email was deleted, the sender would receive an email similar to I am on holiday. I cannot read your email. Your email is being deleted. Please contact Markus or Linda if it's an urgent matter or re-send the email after I return to the office on November 12.

Both Germany and France have also made moves to rein in employers. In 2014, Germany banned managers from calling or emailing staff after work. More recently, France enacted a law that bans after-work emails.

However, if you are telecommuting and working across time zones, it can be hard to unplug, especially if there are no laws protecting your work-life balance. Nonetheless, it's as important, or perhaps more important, for you to do so.

7.3 Set the right boundaries

Beyond being healthy, unplugging gives you clarity and perspective. Unplugging also gives you the space you need to let other thoughts and ideas surface. When you are always on, you don't allow other things to the surface that might be more important.

1. *Notice distractions:* Stop the distractions, get your projects in line. Additionally, it makes you feel more in control of yourself and your life, which has a huge impact on overall happiness. When you find it difficult to unplug, conduct a quick self-assessment:

   - Is it force of habit?
   - Is it because you frequently check social media?

- Is it to deal with FOMO about the latest scoop?
- Is it a form of procrastination?
- Is it because you are frequently behind schedule and forced to put in more hours?

By establishing the reasons you struggle to unplug, you can start to better understand what mental attitude you need to adopt to make time to be offline.

If you're unwilling to unplug for what might be considered workaholic reasons, determine if your work schedule is overloaded or if you are making systematic mistakes that are impacting your efficiency.

Are regular distractions, such as social media or co-workers, interrupting your workflow? Probably. The average worker enjoys no more than three minutes of work without distractions. After an interruption, it takes 25 minutes to refocus, which is detrimental to your efficiency. By establishing what work and life goals you want to prioritize, it's possible to eliminate distractions. To do this, create a list of the top three tasks you want to accomplish for the day, week, and month. If you get those three things done, that day, week or month will be considered productive. Anything you accomplish beyond those is simply a bonus.

2. *Learn to prioritize:* Prioritization also involves knowing what you want out of life, such as physical health or time for your family. Once you've identified what's at the top of your list, you can make adjustments to your life and schedule to make sure they don't end up on a back burner. By knowing your priorities, it is easier to say "no" to distractions that will drain your energy and resources away from what is most important to you.

If you tend to say yes without thinking when you're asked to do something extra, stall. Don't answer straight away. Say you'll get back to the person asking, then use that time to think clearly about whether to say yes or no. If you want to say yes, fine. But if you want to say no, say no and keep saying it. Don't justify your actions or give excuses. There's no need to be nasty or rude.

Saying "no", doesn't mean you have to turn down work. If a task that is going to ruin your workflow and have a negative impact on your priorities for the day pops up out of the blue, tell your coworker or client that you can do the project, but not until tomorrow (or whenever is best for your timeline).

3. *Work Smarter, Not Harder:* The old adage work smarter, not

harder, is more applicable now than ever as distractions through social media and demands on your time continue to exponentially increase. The key to working smarter is strictly managing your time. Do not fall into the trap of multitasking. Multitasking is a work-place myth used to justify constant distractions: both internal and external. The mind can focus on only a little information at any single moment, which means that any attempt to multitask will lead to scatter-brained results. So, focus solely on the task at hand, whether it is putting the final touches on a presentation or tossing around a baseball with your son.

Imposing a strict schedule for your work will provide structure for focus. People often get distracted by emails, so establish set times for checking email, replying only to the ones that merit the time of your response.

4. *The Pomodoro technique:* The Pomodoro technique can also help you create structure in your schedule. It sets aside 25 minutes of your undivided attention for the task at hand. Then, you rest for five minutes. As you become more adept at using the technique, you can slowly increase the time. However, if you reach the point that distractions start slipping in, scale it back.

Given that you can do a full-body workout in as few as seven minutes, it should be no surprise how much work you can accomplish during a focused, 25-minute session. Be just as strict with yourself during your rest time; rest is an important part of the system, as it allows your brain to relax and recover.

5. *Leave on time every day:* The most important step to managing your work schedule, and creating the ideal work-life balance, is to leave work when your working hours are finished. Even if you telecommute, by establishing a clear work space and hours, you can give yourself the same release

from work as anybody sitting in an office. Knowing that you won't start checking work emails at 10 p.m. that night helps keep you focused during working hours. By following these general rules, as well as other productivity techniques, it is possible to work smarter, not harder.

6. *Let go of Perfection:* Many people think that procrastination is caused by a person's laziness, disorganization or apathy, but it couldn't be further from the truth.

Usually, procrastination is caused by one of four reasons:

- Low energy level
- Lack of focus

- Fear of failure or success
- Perfectionism

By this point, you should have some ideas on how to improve your focus, and as you establish a better work-life balance, you'll improve your energy levels. That said, these last two reasons for procrastination can be the downfall of smart, dedicated workers. It can be very hard to let go of perfectionism, especially when it's been ingrained in you as a child. Many overachievers found it easy to balance everything when they were younger, but struggle as they enter the adult world and are looking to find the ideal work-life balance.

Perfectionists face three major issues at work: overworking, failing to delegate, and fear of failure. All of these problems can lead to a snowballing effect of projects piling up on your already full plate.

It's easy to say "let go of perfection", but how do you actually do it?

First, realize that perfectionism is no excuse. If you tell your boss, colleagues, or clients that the delay is because "you want everything to be perfect", you aren't getting any sympathy. Late is late. Second, focus on progress, not perfection. Some perfectionists clam up at the start of a project because they can see the big picture, but don't know how to break it down into smaller steps. It's important to start doing something that moves you toward the end goal, no matter how small that step is.

Lastly, show self-compassion. Forgive yourself and acknowledge that mistakes are part of life. The law of diminishing returns establishes that at a certain point there will still be mistakes, but the energy and time it takes to rectify them no longer outweighs the benefits.

7. *Make Time for Yourself:* You work hard. Give yourself credit for that and treat yourself well. By

incorporating enjoyable forms of exercise into your daily schedule, you will not only be healthier, but you will also have more energy to tackle your work. Say goodbye to overtime and nights at the office.

By working these two practices into a daily routine, they will both become second nature. There will be an adjustment period. However, once you find the rhythm, you'll discover that you enjoy both more and more each day. Beyond regular breaks in the office, such as those prescribed in the Pomodoro technique, take a vacation. While on holiday, allow yourself to shut off your phone and close your laptop so that you can relax and unwind. By letting go while you're on holiday, you're more likely to return to work invigorated and focused.

Finally, don't forget that there is more to your life than sleeping and working. Set aside time in your schedule to take up a hobby. Even the busiest, most successful people pursue hobbies, as they enrich their lives and help bring depth and meaning to what they do.

Your Quick Start Action Step: Track your time

In order to ensure that you can eventually get your work/life balance to the right place, the first thing you are going to need to do is to track how much you are currently working so that you can see where you need to improve. While tracking the amount of time you spend working each week it is important to do so for at least a month and then average out the hours. You should also pick a month that represents the full variety of your tasks if possible. During this time it is also important to ensure that you work as you would normally without doing anything out of the ordinary that would affect your results. After all, if you skew the results then the only person you are going to be hurting is yourself.

If you work a salaried position, then this should be a relatively easy step as it becomes about not letting your employer take undue advantage of you. If you are an hourly or freelance employee, however, then this step will also require that you sit down and put together a budget based on the amount of work you currently do as well as the amount of work you would be doing if you adjusted your work/life balance accordingly. While it can be tempting to work as much as possible, especially if you are a freelancer and the work isn't always available, making a change may be easier if you look at it as making taking a hit in the short-term in exchange for a prolonged amount of work you can do effectively in the long-term as you won't have to worry about mental clutter.

Chapter 8:
Remaining in the Moment
at Work

Chapter 8: Remaining in the Moment at Work

8.1 The Sad Truth

For many people, the work day is a time for lots of stress, with little left over when it comes to mitigating it properly. Mindfulness is a great choice for use during the work day not just for the ways it helps decrease the symptoms of depression, anxiety, and stress but also for the ways it can help you focus on the task at hand. In addition, the boost to empathy will make you more liked around the office in addition to being more efficient.

Practicing mindfulness at work can help you turn your reactions into reasoned responses. A reaction is a nearly automatic action which takes place in response to a set of stimuli while a response comes to a stimulus after a thorough assessment of the situation. If you spend enough time in the moment, then a moment starts to feel like more than enough time to come to a reasonable solution.

Practicing mindfulness can also train you to come at new problems in a different way. First, it is important to instead think of the problems as challenges to be met. A challenge is something that can be bested and learned from, two things that being mindful prepares you for quite readily. Consider writing down the challenge and spending a few moments focusing on it and its solutions, odds are you will then find it much easier to come up with a solution.

8.2 **A Net Positive**

While not possible with all professions, with practice you will find that you can squeeze in a few minutes of mindfulness meditation here and there throughout the day. While the individual efficacy of any particular mindfulness meditation session might be relatively minimal, the overall gestalt will lead to a sense of wellbeing that is greater than the sum of its overall parts. While it might seem difficult to deal with the demands of the day, the demands of your coworkers and everything else that life throws at you, you can consider each micro mindfulness meditation session as islands of calm in an otherwise choppy sea. Mindfulness in the workplace should be thought of as a tool that allows you to squeeze every bit of efficiency out of the workday as long as you think carefully about how to use it as effectively as possible.

While it might seem that making an effort to practice mindfulness in the office will lead to an overall decrease in productivity, the reality is that the opposite is true. Especially if you have a particularly hectic job you likely find that you often have to react to things without thinking through all the possible outcomes of your response. With your head cleared from frequent micro-meditations, however, you will find that the moments in which you have to make important decisions naturally seem to expand in order to provide you with all the time you need to make the right choice, right now.

Remember, when you react to something you at taking a nearly automatic action, letting the stimuli that sent you down this path take control of the situation. However, if you respond instead of react, then you are making a well-reasoned choice based on all available data. Reasoned responses lead to better solutions every single time.

8.3 **Getting Started**

Mindfulness in the workplace should be used as a tool for the purpose of squeezing out every last bit of efficiency from the day that you can, by ensuring you think as carefully about how to use it productively as possible. If you are already using your commute to practice mindfulness, then when you arrive at work you will already be in a mindful state that will allow you to get the most out of each moment. In order to keep the mindfulness train rolling, you will want to take a moment or two between tasks in order to focus on your breathing and thus the sensory data that your body is providing.

This doesn't need to be the sort of elaborate process that you learned to complete at home, it should only take a minute or two to ensure your head remains on straight throughout the day. Quantity trumps quality in this situation and if you practice each time you switch tasks you will find that your early-morning mindfulness state persists throughout the day. This is not to say that you fail if you can't take a moment to be mindful between every set of tasks, as long as you fit it in when and where you can, you will come out streets ahead in the long-term.

For many people, clearing their mind during the work day can be extremely difficult. If your job leaves you little time to sneak in a bit of mindfulness, then simply start with whatever you can get, even if it is just 30 seconds. Over time, you will get a feel for when you can sneak in 30 seconds of solace and learn the best way to chain dozens, if not hundreds together throughout the day.

Clearing your mind in the middle of the work day can be tricky, but like with all type of mindfulness, each time you do so will make the next time that much easier. Don't push yourself unreasonably, however, starting with just a few micro mediations each day is still a great effort in the right direction. If you work in an office, any time you need a moment to catch your breath, and you want that moment to last as long as possible, consider the following. Otherwise, alter it for your situation as needed.

1. As you breathe in and out normally, be aware of the breath in your lungs before expanding that awareness outward.

2. Become aware of your fingers as they glide across the keyboard in front of you, listen to the sound of the keys pressing as you go about your business. Focus on the decision to press each key and

the resulting actions that come into play because of it.

3. Focus on your body, straightening your posture to its ideal limits and taking in the sensations being given off by the lower half of your body.

4. Take one more breath and let the rest of the world back in to continue on about your day as normal.

Additionally, any time you find yourself in a meeting or a particularly long conversation with a coworker you can use the opportunity to slip into a mindful mindset by simply focusing on what the other person is saying to the exclusion of everything else that is going on around you. Remember, being mindful isn't about being choosy when it comes to which moments you are fully present in, it is about embracing the now in all its many forms.

If you spend a large portion of your day either responding to smartphone notification or emails, then you can find some time to practice mindfulness by simply taking 30 seconds between each reply to center yourself and briefly be mindful. While 30 seconds might not seem like much, you will be surprised at how powerful the cumulative effect can be. Think about it this way, if you respond to 100 email or notifications in a day then you are really giving yourself nearly an hour each day in which to be mindful. Once you give it a try, you will likely find it hard to give up.

If your job requires that you sit in one place for most of the day then it is also important to double check on your posture before you get started. You can do this by relaxing all of your muscles, starting with your neck and extending the exercise all the way down to your toes. You will then want to reverse things and go the other way, starting at the bottom and working your way back up to your neck. After you are relaxed you should find that you are more easily able to handle the signals that your body is sending out, making it easier for you to determine if you have any pain points you have been ignoring that you can easily deal with.

If your job fins you repeating the same more or less mindless task throughout the day then you can use this opportunity to practice mindfulness. Any activity that includes a physical activity as well as the need to focus on one thing in what is more or less a passive way is a great way to set yourself up for a mindful experience. All you need to do is to put all of your focus on the task at hand and you should be able to spend your day in a mindful state.

In order to maximize the effectiveness of your end of day commute and the mindfulness meditation you are hopeful going to practice during that time, you should take the last five minutes of the work day to put aside everything that has happened, both good and bad, while you were on the clock. During this time you will want to think about all of the things you have been able to accomplish, as well as those things which you had to put off until tomorrow and even the things you just plain missed the boat on. You will then want to consider all of this in light of the bigger picture and thing about what it all means long-term. Finally, with the day truly done you will then want to close the door on it and leave any unsolved problems alone until tomorrow. Remind yourself that tomorrow is another day and let yourself move on with your day free from your work day cares.

Quick action step

The best way to ensure that you can continue to be mindful throughout the work day is to take steps to help yourself develop a mindful mindset before you even get to the office. A great way to do so is by commuting mindfully.

Start as soon as you get into your vehicle by vocalizing your intention to be mindful during your morning commute. Then take a few deep breaths and use this time to become more aware of your body. Become aware of your hands on the steering wheel and what they feel beneath them. Become aware of your body and the sensations it feels as it is pressed against your seat. Feel your foot on the pedal and the resistance it feels as you prepare to drive. As you begin your drive take in the world around you while at the same time striving to be aware of the act of seeing, of the act of hearing. Try to focus on these three things, body, sights, sounds and only these things for the length of your drive.

That's really all there is to it, though like many things it is much easier said than done. Today's society is obsessed with multi-tasking and as such your mind will want to wander, thoughts will try and sneak their way in, you will want to think about the things waiting for you at work or tasks you left unfinished at home. Your phone will make at least one noise and you will be tempted to see the specifics of the notification. It is important to ignore these obstacles. Likewise, it is important to not dwell on these thoughts or distractions that are given into as that is, in reality, another thought trying to sneak its way in. Instead, you must acknowledge the errant thought or temptation and let it go without interacting with it further. Over time you will find that the process of existing at the moment will become easier while also noticing a wide variety of additional benefits as well.

Chapter 9: Home Management 101: How to Effectively Declutter Your Home

Chapter 9: Home Management 101: How to Effectively Declutter Your Home

9.1 **Face the facts**

Not many of us are natural minimalists. Plenty of us are more, let's say, maximalists. Clutter seems to be magnetically attracted to us and honestly, we're secretly waiting for a knock on the door from the producers of the show *Hoarders*. That's why it can be quite a relief sometimes when it comes time to move someplace new. Finally, you're forced to go through all of your possessions with a fine-tooth comb, and you have the chance to really clean up your act by giving your whole household a thorough decluttering service.

Keeping only the things you love or that are useful and getting rid of things you no longer need or want, helps you create a life that is more streamlined. And it allows you to live in a home where you can find things more easily and where you'll spend less time constantly tidying up piles of accumulated belongings.

The bonus of giving your household a decluttering service right before you move is that you will have fewer items to pack and transport, and so the whole moving process will be faster, easier and cheaper. Even if this is not the case, however, you will still find that decluttering your home is worth the effort.

9.2 **Less can be more**

A study by Pamela Thacher, assistant professor of psychology at St. Lawrence University in Canton, N.Y., found that people who sleep in cluttered rooms... are more likely to have sleeping problems. This includes having trouble falling asleep at night and experiencing rest disturbances. Additionally, people who make their beds every morning experience longer, more restful sleep, especially when they use fresh, clean sheets.

Researchers at the University of Minnesota found that people who spent time in an unorganized room were twice as likely to eat a chocolate bar than an apple. And researchers at Florida State University reveal a link between hoarding and obesity, noting that people with extremely cluttered homes are 77% more likely to be overweight.

If you start to minimalize your possessions, you open your home up to all kinds of potential that you may not have seen while the home was cluttered. You will be able to find everything that you need with minimal effort, allowing you to devote more time to living life to the fullest. You will also understand that filling the home up with junk isn't productive or valuable because it takes away that freedom and not only that – it costs money.

Imagine being able to access a cupboard or closet and find what you want straight away. Imagine being able to leave a room as clean as it was when you entered it. It sounds clinical and cold to some people but in fact, they may be kidding themselves into a false sense of security because the truth is these spaces don't have to be cold. They can, in fact, be welcoming because they encourage the mind to work with more than the stuff that is in the home. This stuff has become a talking point between people but when you take it away, true conversation flows that is meaningful.

Express yourself: You get a chance to express your own creativity instead of having it imposed upon you by all of your possessions and you begin to remember what life is all about and change your values. Your focus will not be on keeping the house clean and tidy. It will do that almost on its own. That means your focus can be used on creativity, enjoyment, and leisure. That gives you more time, more money, less stress, and a more abundant lifestyle! See how less can be more?

You'll spend less money: When a major goal of your style of living is to have less stuff, it's almost guaranteed that you're going to end up spending less money on goods, products or services. With the internet at our fingertips, it can sometimes be difficult to curb our spending. Along these same lines, another common mode of thought is the idea that if you make more money, then all of your financial problems will go away. When you chase more and more money, your consumption often becomes more and more problematic. One day you'll look around and think that you have it all; a large house, a fancy car, and lots of stuff that fits inside of your lovely consumption-driven life. What you'll most likely be missing is substance and a sense of joy. Don't allow these ideals to dominate your lifestyle. Spend less, own little tangible goods, and lead the happiest life that you can. It's that simple.

Reduce your stress: Stress can cause physical ailments in the sense that it contributes to premature aging, those pesky grey hairs on your head, and even memory loss. What's more, clutter in the home is known to shift our attention away from what we are truly trying to focus on. We have enough stressors in our life; we don't need our stuff to provide with more reasons to worry.

If you want to test your own reaction to how you react to clutter in your home, you can try this small experiment. Find one messy countertop in your home (this may be easier for some people than others). Next, take the time to really clean off another countertop in your home. After you've done this, look at each countertop separately and gauge your internal reaction to each one. It's probably not surprising that you are most likely going to find that the clean countertop is going to provide you with a sense of calm, while the messy countertop is going to shoot some kind of stress indicator into your brain and body.

9.3 Keep, sell, throw

1. *Overview:* There are many ways to successfully purge. Some

decluttering experts advocate the Four Box Method, where the idea is to go through each room in your home, armed with separate boxes: one for things you want to keep, one for items to sell or give to charity, one for things to chuck, and one box for things you're still undecided about.

Others are devotees of the Japanese KonMari method, where you pick up each item you own and decide to keep it only if it "sparks joy" or if it is useful. There's even "Swedish death cleaning", a new decluttering technique where you downsize your belongings in recognition of the stark fact that one day, you won't be able to take anything with you, and that your junk will only be a burden for your loved ones. But hey, if that's too much for you, you might prefer to stick with the Four Box Method.

Whatever method you use, most decluttering experts advise tackling only one room at a time, rather than attempting to declutter your whole house in one go. Give yourself enough time to ensure you don't stress out and become overwhelmed with the magnitude of the job. But if you're moving soon, and want to get it all done asap, don't be afraid to call in help from a professional decluttering service, which can be surprisingly affordable. Experts advise tackling only one room at a time, rather than attempting to declutter your whole house in one go.

2. *Get a friend to help:* As shows like *Hoarders* have demonstrated, the problem is usually with our psychological attachment to objects, rather than there being any physical difficulty in picking up items and placing them in boxes or garbage bags. Sometimes, what you really need is a truly objective person to help you with the task of discerning trash from treasure. That's where hiring someone who offers a decluttering service can make things so much easier.

Don't mistake the idea of a decluttering service as involving a stranger coming in and charging about, dumping your prized possessions in rubbish bags with reckless abandon. It can be as harmless as having an assistant follow you around, taking your directions, but also being critical enough to say.

Or you may go the whole hog and engage someone to assist you with a full decluttering service by completely reorganizing all your belongings, room by room: sorting and tidying and removing excess clutter–with your approval naturally.

Your helper can undertake all kinds of decluttering tasks, like organizing your DVD and CD libraries, or rearranging your kitchen cupboards and pantry or reorganizing your clothes. They can also be tasked with making repeated trips to dispose of junk. And in the end, once you are sitting in a beautiful, tidy, organized home, you'll find packing up for your move and unpacking in your new house an absolute breeze.

We're all familiar with the mantra 'a place for everything and everything in its place', even if that place is concealed beneath a million other absolutely essential objects. In recent years, a whole industry has built up to encourage us to rid ourselves of possessions that clog up our lives or, at least, our hallways.

3. *Objects must 'spark joy:* 'Spark joy' is the phrase that launched 1,000 skips. It comes from *The Life-Changing Magic of Tidying Up*, written by Japanese decluttering guru Marie Kondo, which has sold more than five million copies. One of the reasons that attempts to declutter stutter, stall and then fail is that books and websites assume we can breezily ditch a lifetime of memories and possessions between walking the dog and breakfast. They don't adequately acknowledge that, if you live in a house filled with

cherished inherited and acquired objects, it's incredibly daunting. It's easy to ditch an Ikea chest of drawers, yet not so easy to get rid of the ormolu cabinet you inherited but hate.

4. *Decide if you are a collector or a discarder:* Your brain is hardwired to be a collector or a discarder. Here lies the first stumbling block. Grandpa's desk is much harder to send off to the auction house than any old desk. Just as you should never name a pig you intend to eat, if you are to surround ourselves only with the things we love, we need to stop giving our possessions names. Try to think of it as the desk or, better yet, simply a desk.

It's not really about the thing, is it? For example, if you have a hideous cut-glass bowl that belonged to your grandmother and it's the shape of a grape, quite the most unpleasant thing, but you'll never get rid of it. To throw it away would be like throwing away the memory of her. That doesn't seem right, does it?

5. *Own your own space:* Throwing away things that are tied in with your memories of people absolutely fine it's really important to own your own space and not have other people's stuff invading it. Things have memories vested in them, but if they're not actually giving you pleasure, then

let them go. When it comes to tackling those important family pieces that inspire more guilt than love, your first step should be to offer it to other members of the family. You look generous and it mitigates guilt. And it's telling if nobody else wants it, isn't it?'

Ultimately, a soothing, peaceful, happy-to-get-up-in house is what it's all about. Keep your eye on that prize and get cracking. You have nothing to lose but (someone else's) junk.

Your Quick Start Action Step: Take it slow

- Start small, with a drawer, a cupboard or a heap of

photographs. Each small success is incredibly motivating.

- Banish thoughts of perfectionism. It's crippling and holds you back. Do what you can. Keep going.

- Declutter first, shop second. Tempting as it is to dash out and buy boxes, cartons and crates, it's displacement activity for the gritty business of throwing things out.

- Don't wait until you can get everyone in your house on board. If necessary, allow the permanently messy a limited area in which to express themselves. Fly-tying kit in the study – yes. All over the kitchen table – no.

- You can get rid of wedding presents and still remain married in the eyes of the law.

Chapter 10:
Choosing a 'Less is More' Lifestyle for Worry-Free and Stress-Free Living

Chapter 10: Choosing a 'Less is More' Lifestyle for Worry-Free and Stress-Free Living

10.1 **Take the plunge**

Minimalism is one of those concepts, like "eating healthy" or "being a good person" that has a somewhat different meaning depending on who you ask. This is perfectly natural, as adhering to a minimalist lifestyle is a personal choice that means something different to everyone who makes it. Again, while your personal mileage might vary when it comes to this definition, many people believe that minimalism is the focused elevation of the things that matter most in life, coupled with the discarding of everything that prevents you from focusing on those things on the first list. More simply put, it is about understanding what is most important to you and acting on that knowledge to the best of your ability.

Living your life in an intentional way is a core part of living a minimalist lifestyle which includes considering the values in life you feel matter the most and then doing everything you can to align your life in such a way that these values take up your time as well as your space. This is precisely why minimalism will look different to everyone because if you ask 100 different people what they would prioritize most, you would get 100 different answers.

There are two different ways to look at this lack of specificity. On one hand, it can be difficult to know if you are starting off on the right foot because the first step is going to be different for everyone. On the other hand, however, it means you can create the unique minimalism framework that is right for you.

Minimalism was a style that actually started coming into popularity in the 1950s. The intention of minimalism is not to do your best to live without anything you want or need. Instead, it is an opportunity to free yourself from material possessions. Through living the minimalist lifestyle, you can attain freedom from: fear, worry, overwhelm, guilt, depression, feeling trapped, and more. As a minimalist, you are not required to throw away nearly all of your belongings and live in a constant state of lack. Instead, it is about learning not to give your material items more value than what they're actually worth in life.

10.2 **Free yourself**

As you adhere to the minimalist lifestyle, you will start to notice long-term effects settle in. These symptoms are pretty much always positive.

People who live the minimalist lifestyle for a while generally note that they feel burden-free. They don't feel a constant responsibility to look after an obscene number of items that they cannot care for, either due to lack of time or lack of desire to. They do not feel guilty for letting things they "should" like sit unused and unappreciated. They do not feel depressed when they look around and see stuff everywhere that is being unused, or not cared for. Instead, they feel completely burden-free! They do not need to spend any more time worrying about, accounting for, or looking after stuff. Instead, they can spend their free time, emotions, and money doing things they love!

When you don't have a significant number of items to look after, you can really feel free! You no longer have to account for so many items, which means you can literally do anything. If you want to move to a new city, state, or even country, you don't have to worry about moving vehicles or packing. Instead, you can fit everything in a suitcase, or a couple of suitcases and just go! You don't have to feel like you have to return home for your stuff, or anything at all! Instead, you can demand your life.

Having a lot of stuff and being in the "rat race" to get more can be exhausting. You can get lost in the feeling like you have to work more to get more stuff, which means you're constantly working and never enjoying yourself. You can also get lost in the constant need to clean and maintain all of your belongings. All of this together can really take up all of your time!

10.3 **Avoid falling back into old habits**

As so much of the modern world is based around consumerist culture, it is important to understand that, as a minimalist, you will constantly be bombarded with advertising designed to make you go against your beliefs. As such, it is important to do everything in your power in order to avoid falling back into bad habits.

1. *Keep your eye on the goal:* Look back to how badly your life was affected by materialism and one thing that does enthuse clients of mine to keep to their new lifestyle is taking photographs of their cluttered lives and then taking new photos of the minimalist

lifestyle. These should be enough to remind you of how you became a slave to things and allowed those things to take priority over your happiness, your ability to see beyond these things and have an impact on your spiritual and moral self.

2. *Say positive things each day about the lifestyle that you have chosen:* Let the light into your home and never look back because it's easy to keep to this lifestyle because it is so user friendly. You don't have to waste so much of your life on housework and being a slave to material demands. You don't let life dictate what makes you happy. You have realized that looking back at the way you were

and comparing it with how you are now, you get a clear picture of the contrasts. Personal happiness and satisfaction will always win over the confusion of mixed messages caused by materialism.

3. *Try affirmations and mantras:* Affirmations or mantras, positive sentences which are repeated throughout the day, are a great way to ensure that you stay on the straight and narrow. Affirmations are written down while mantras are repeated either aloud or in your head and both make it easier to block out any negative static that your fixed mindset has to contribute in a given situation.

Common mantras and affirmations include things like:

- I can follow my path to happiness no matter how rocky it may be
- Success is measured in forwarding progress
- Through hard work, I can attract the love and success I deserve
- I am strong enough to overcome any obstacle
- I can find fulfilment through dedication and perseverance

To ensure you don't bite off more than you can chew all at once, it is recommended that you start off with an affirmation or mantra that is fairly close to your current mental comfort zone. Starting with something small will make it easier to rewire your brain in a positive direction when compared to starting with something serious right off the bat.

When using mantras and affirmations for the first time it is common for your fixed mindset to actively rebel against them. This means you may feel stupid for writing or thinking them or feel the urge to give up early on because the activity seems pointless. This is just all of the negative filters in your mind trying to do their job and keep you doing whatever it is that you have been doing. While it will be difficult to appreciate in the moment, the fact that they are acting up really just means that they are working which means you should really be pleased as opposed to annoyed. Instead it is important to keep in mind that success will not appear overnight as it will take time for your new and improved mindset to stick. You should feel as though it is easier to keep it up as you go along, however, which should be a fine indicator of your success overall.

If you find that your mindset is more fixed than most and your best efforts don't seem to be making a dent in your negative mentality then you may be trying to make too big of a change all at once. If this is the case then your mantras and affirmations may not be getting through to your psyche regardless of how frequently you use them. If you feel as though this might be the case with you then you may want to dial back the overall positivity of your statements until your brain starts to get the hang of things. Starting with a mild change should be enough to grease the wheels of progress and help you ultimately build to something that can generate serious results.

Once you banish your negative thoughts it will be time to replace them with positive alternatives instead. It is important to have a general idea of what these will be from the start to ensure you don't fill the void with something that ends up being on par, or worse, than what you are replacing.

To get started all you need to do is look inside yourself and consider what exactly you want the end result to be. Once you know what this goal is, the next thing you are going to need to do is ask yourself why you want to make the change in question and how it is going to benefit you in both the short and the long-term. You should strive to always have a larger purpose in mind when setting these goals as it will be far easier to follow through even when the going gets tough.

When you get ready to make a change of this magnitude it is vital that you understand that much of the journey is going to be uphill and the progress will be very slow going. While working towards your goals it is thus crucial to take note of the triggers you were dealing with during your fixed mindset days in order to ensure they don't follow you to your growth mindset phase and end up negating all of your hard work before you even get started. As long as you are aware of what these triggers are then you should be able to successfully avoid them.

4. *Fully commit:* In order to ever hope to see results, you are going to need to dedicate yourself to the idea completely, this means following through without

reservation to ensure that your day to day reactions are always on message with what it is that you are striving towards. Making a decision to commit fully to the task at hand will go a long way towards silencing your inner critic. If you don't commit fully, you then ultimately run the risk of falling back into negative habits after months, or even years, and destroying all your hard work.

5. *Understand your triggers:* When it comes to maintaining successfully, it is important to keep in mind are the things that might make you lose control and revert to your bad habits. Understanding your triggers will then help you to understand the

habits that they prop up which will make them easier to avoid in the future.

While you may not be able to think of many of your triggers right off the bat, if you go throughout your week and make a list of every time you did something that was actively against your currently stated goal of the moment then you will be on the right track. You will then want to consider what it is that you have come up with and how you can go about mitigating those triggers, at least until you have gotten the concept of self-discipline under control.

Once you have chosen a mantra or affirmation that is right for you, it is important that you utilize it to the fullest. This means you will want to ensure that it is the first thing you think in the morning when you wake up, and then once and hour, on the hour, throughout the rest of the day, before making sure it is the last thing you think before you fall asleep at night. When working through it, ensure that you really focus on the words, to the exclusion of all else.

Your Quick Start Action Step: Don't Go Alone

Starting any major life journey on your own will always prove to be more difficult than if you have someone there cheering you on! The minimalist community is amazing and can be extremely helpful to on the days in which you find it difficult to look past the process of decluttering to a future filled with more time, more money, and more attention for the people you love.

Chapter 11:
Taking it to the
Next Level with a
Tiny House

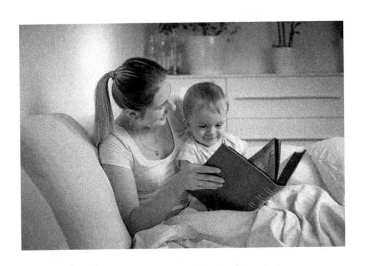

Chapter 11: Taking it to the Next Level with a Tiny House

10.1 How Tiny is Tiny?

A new trend has arisen, known as tiny house living. It is a great example of minimalism, because with this type of living, you have to have the minimal amount of stuff, because you do not have the space to have a lot of stuff. You also get really close to your family as well, because you have to learn how to coexist in less than eight hundred square feet of space. This new trend has come about due to some states making tiny houses to give to the homeless that live there, so that they have a place to live, a place they can call their own.

Once people saw that you can live comfortably in a really small house if it is built right, they wanted to reduce their living space, and give it a try. There are so many options for tiny house living, and some options are really simple, such as living in a camper. Some people have a tiny house built for them as well, and these ones are a lot more complex than just living in a camper.

Tiny house living is a trend where people live in a dwelling that is less than eight hundred square feet of space. Some people argue that it has become even smaller, and to be considered a tiny house it has to be less than five hundred square feet of space. These people are known as extremists. Because a family of five would have a hard time squeezing into anything less than seven hundred square feet. However, if you are a smaller family, then it is generally not considered tiny house living until you reach five hundred or less.

There are many different ways to do tiny house living. Some people get a small camper, and they live in it. A camper is great if you want to be mobile and travel the world, or even if you just want to cut down on utility bills, because most campsites will cut you a good deal if you live there year-round. Most campsites you can get a deal where if you pay up front for the whole month, it is only 200 dollars a month. Or, better yet, you can get a job as a camp host and live there year-round for free. Living in a camper is not that bad, as you have a bathroom in most, a kitchen, beds, a table and a living space where you can put up a television.

Often times, the kitchen table and the couch in the living area also turn into beds, so you have extra sleeping space. You can get close to nature, and you can sure save a lot of money, especially if you become a camp host. You can't have a whole lot of stuff either, because there just is not space for it, which makes it great for minimalism.

You could turn a shed into a tiny house. This is what a lot of people do, as they find sheds are pretty cheap to purchase, and it doesn't take much to get them up to code. You can even find sheds already wired and ready for electricity, all you have to do is add plumbing, which for such a small space would not take a lot of money, because with a tiny space like that it is ideal to have the bathroom and the kitchen ran on the same wall. You can find sheds that have porches and doors like a little house, and some even come with lofts already built in for your bedroom. It is almost as if these sheds were built for tiny house living, when in reality they used to be used for little shops or play houses for kids. Another good thing about these sheds is that they are easily moved, and you can even make them mobile on their own by welding an old trailer frame to them and adding wheels. Then you can travel with it as if it were a camper. The great thing about these tiny sheds is that you can install solar panels on them for fairly cheap if you make them yourself, and it does not take many to power the entire place.

Another option is to build your own tiny home. This has some downsides and some upsides. The downside is, most of the time if you build your own, it has to be stationary due to coding reasons in most states. You cannot make it mobile, so you would have to find a space to settle down and build there. Another downside is it can be kind of expensive if you add a lot of amenities to your tiny house, such as sliding walls to make it seem like you have more space because when you aren't using the kitchen, you can just slide it into the wall, same with the bath room and bedrooms. The upsides are plenty though.

You can make the house just as you want it, so you know you are getting the most out of the space that you have. You can make it the most energy efficient possible. This is a good thing, because you can save money on utilities. You can even completely remove your need for electricity if you use solar panels. So then you would only have to pay the city for sewage, water and trash. Plus you can make your tiny house entirely electric so you won't need a gas bill either. This can save you over two hundred dollars a month on utilities alone. Plus if you keep the bill down on building your tiny home, then you can save money that way as well.

You can also buy pre-made tiny homes. There are ones that are built into the ground, and they are called hobbit homes. They get their design from the home that Bilbo Baggins lives in in the Hobbit trilogy. You can plant a garden on top of your home, and they are completely reliant on renewable energy. You can also buy tiny homes that look like tiny homes. These tiny homes also are generally installed with solar panels, and they can be put wherever you like. These too are meant to be stationary though, so you have to be sure of where you want to live.

10.2 Why People Choose Tiny Living

There are many different reasons to choose living in a tiny home. A lot of people find it comforting to be so close to their family, and to have a space that is cozy. Here are the benefits to living in a tiny house.

1. *Less Stuff:* Living in a tiny home makes it impossible to accumulate a lot of stuff. You have to make sure that everything you have you absolutely need, because if you do not need it, it will just clutter up your little home, so to avoid

clutter, you get rid of a lot of your stuff. This helps you shift your focus to your family, and away from devices that you really don't need.

2. *Closeness:* Think about your family now. When was the last time your kids came to you for advice? Which parent do they bother more? Do they talk to either parent really at all? When was the last time everyone sat down to dinner and talked about their day? With tiny house living, you have to communicate with your family because you are all pretty much on top of each other twenty four/seven. This is great for when your kids hit their teenage years, because they cannot run off and shut

themselves in their rooms and ignore the world. They have to come to you for advice.

If they have lived the tiny house lifestyles most of their life, they will end up wanting to come to you for advice, because they will be use to the closeness you all share as a family. This will create a bond between you and your children and help them grow up and turn into secure adults, because they will know for sure that you are there for them. Sure, in the beginning going from a large space to a tiny one can be aggravating, but if you stick with it, you will begin to love the fact that you are in the same room with your family all day, because it opens the gates of communication. Think about it. How awkward would it be to sit in the same room with them day in and day out in silence? Pretty awkward. So you are forced to communicate, and eventually the house will be filled with laughter and joy.

3. *Simplicity:* There is something amazing about just sitting back and enjoying life, not worried about having a whole huge house to clean. Life is a whole lot easier when it only takes twenty minutes to clean the entire house. You also find that you get in a better routine of picking things up in order to keep your sanity in check, because tiny houses get cluttered

easily. Life is easier in a tiny house, and in some ways, it is a lot better.

10.3 How Tiny Houses Equal Minimalism

Tiny houses are a type of minimalism to be honest. You are minimizing everything, including your living space. Think about it. You can't have a lot of junk if you have nowhere to store it. In a tiny house you have to have the minimum of everything, from clothes, to dishes. Everything has to be taken in moderation. That is what minimalism is. Less is more, and you can get along just fine without all the gadgets and gizmos that the world says you have to have.

Tiny house living is a great form of minimalism because it is tangible minimalism. You actually feel that you are living the lifestyles, rather than just following some guidelines, and this is a great thing, because it can make you want to spread the word all over the world. This is an amazing feeling and can spread like the flu to others as well.

Think about it. You are moving from a house that is probably over a thousand square feet into something that is less than five hundred square feet. That is a big difference. You are going from a large dining room table, a roomy living room with a large recliner, long couch, and a love seat all around a large flat screen television. To a room that houses your living, dining, and cooking space. You leave behind a giant refrigerator and downsize to a small apartment sized or smaller refrigerator. You go from having enough dishes to serve a small army to having just enough dishes to serve your family. You downsize on clothes, keeping only what you wear on a regular basis, and getting rid of all of the rest. You go from having kitchen gadgets galore, to only having a stove, and maybe a toaster and microwave.

You get rid of anything you do not absolutely need. You go from a house full of stuff, most of which you haven't messed with in months or more, to the bare necessities. Not much more than a bed, the clothes on your back, and the food in your stomach. Everything else goes. Yet, you will find, that you couldn't be happier, because you are away from the stress of having too much stuff.

Your Quick Start Action Step: Don't Go Alone

When was the last time you went camping? How did it make you feel? Chances are, you felt at peace, and you never wanted to leave. That is because you were experiencing a small dose of minimalism, and just that small dose was enough to leave you wanting more. Minimalism does work, and tiny house living is a lot like permanent camping. You may find that you never want to live in a large house again.

Bonus Chapter: Getting Rid of Digital Clutter to Maximize Technology Use and Simplifying Your Life

SOCIAL MEDIA

Bonus Chapter: Getting Rid of Digital Clutter to Maximize Technology Use and Simplifying Your Life

12.1 **Know your enemy**

Digital clutter is a sneaky thing. Unlike the surplus gadgets in your kitchen, data hides on your computer, your smartphone, and in the cloud. It also festers within your credit card purchase history, schoolwork, medical records, driver's abstract, and any legal proceedings you've been party to. Yet much of this information is largely invisible. Sure, you walk by your computer daily or pick up your smartphone frequently but the information within is in a nice tidy package. Only when you start looking for something specific are you likely to realize that you have too many emails, digital photographs, or other files. The volume and variety of information can be a burden in ways you might not even realize.

Whether you like it or not, digital clutter is inevitable. Only the most diligent have taken time to be rigorous about deleting old files, organizing current files, and so on. More often the solution is to buy more storage to house an ever growing data collection. This chapter will explore the kinds of data in your life, and strategies to help you manage your information. Think of it as a digital cleanse.

Digital decluttering is the process of organizing your data and technology in ways that support your lifestyle. To get started, you need to be clear on what digital clutter is and why decluttering is important to you. In this part, we'll explore the digital clutter problem, the benefits of digital decluttering, and how the process
works.

Online technologies have evolved and changed our lives at home and in the office at a dramatic pace over the past 30 years. The rate at which we've adopted new technologies and improvements to Internet upload and download speeds are impressive. Add to that the evolution from pagers to smartphones and the increased power of the computer for even more change.

However, all that change has created a problem: Digital clutter.

Before we dive in, it may be helpful to pause a moment and consider what digital cluttering means to you. How do you define it? How does digital clutter make you feel? How does it impact your life?

Digital clutter is a fairly new problem. Our ancestors may have lived with too many objects but they didn't live with the same volume of information. By ancestors, we only have to look one generation back. Some grew up with analog information and have had to adapt to digital living while others were born into the digital life. For both groups, digital clutter is an artifact of the Internet, personal computers, social networking, and smart devices. We now consciously create and unconsciously contribute to terabytes of data every year.

Our personal collection of data started slowly. With home and office computers, work previously done by hand or with typewriters and adding machines moved into word processing and spreadsheet software. Files were stored on floppy disks and rudimentary hard drives. In 1993, there were about 600 websites. Early Internet adopters may have accessed those first websites, a few Bulletin Board System (BBS) message boards and, possibly, had an ICQ identity. I seek you, remember?

Flash forward and today we live with what too much data smog

We have millions of websites and years' worth of YouTube videos to watch plus social networking and cloud storage. Add to that our mobile phones, tablets, laptops, and smart home devices. We have vast search histories and medical, financial, and shopping digital records. And let's not forget any lingering remnants of data from our older collections of USB drives, SD cards, and defunct computers. Think back to when you first started using a computer. How much data have you created since then? How much information have you accessed?

To quantify that data think in terabytes (TB). You know, bytes, kilobytes, megabytes, gigabytes, terabytes, and so on. The Register recently quoted a Western Digital Corporation finding that the "average US household has 41.5 TB of data spread across 14 digital devices, and this is only going to grow"

That 41.5 TB can hold more than 1 million hours of 1080 HD video or nearly 21 million digital photos of 2 MB each or trillions of pages of text. That's just the average per household!

Unfortunately, we spend a lot of our time just clearing the junk, which we're now forced to do in order to discover anything we might actually care about. By sheer volume alone, everyone needs to do some data decluttering.

12.2 Benefits of Digital Decluttering

No matter its origins, digital information is central to our way of living today. As a result, we've got to take ownership of our digital footprint. Beyond simply clearing the clutter, there are many benefits.

Better organization means efficiency and, if time is money, it improves your bottom line. By knowing what information you have and where to find it, you can make the most of your time both online and offline. In doing so, you reduce the amount of information you have to process — what psychologists call "cognitive load"— and self-administer the antidote to information overwhelm.

That recovered time and reduced cognitive load can be used to nurture your interests and try new things. Furthermore, reducing the digital noise around you minimizes distractions and creates space to focus on more complex projects, including analog projects away from your computer.

Digital decluttering also creates space for self-care. Taking control of the amount of time you spend online allows you to focus on what's important to you. Time away from the screen is the best prevention for "sitting disease," a term I first heard from the pelvic health specialist, Kim Vopni. Less screen time can also improve your sleep patterns, protect your hearing, and give your eyes a much needed rest.

That same self-care space allows you to nourish meaningful relationships, reigniting your listening skills and ability to focus. Genuine connections are often lost in the digital clutter and rekindling the skills to foster those connections benefit all. If you're a parent or other role model for children and youth, demonstrating the healthy use of technology is one of the best ways to pass on this digital life lesson.

In addition to the practical, physical, and social benefits of digital decluttering, you may find peace in other aspects of your life. Understanding your data and how you use technology can highlight the myths of the perfectly polished life. What is published online is often a curated collection of posts that perpetuate the myth of the perfect life. Knowing this can reduce envy and your need to "keep up with the Joneses."

Similarly, understanding your data can help you find the elements that are key in your quest for digital happiness. If you love taking photographs, then take photographs! If Instagram Stories make you happy, then create and view them. However, you should strive to put strategies in place to put boundaries around your use of technology so that the digital parts of your life are fulfilling, not draining.

Digital decluttering can also be a good reminder of the privilege of digital access. Not all sectors of society nor all places in the world have such ready access to technology and information. By noting this privilege, we can be appreciative of the opportunity rather than burdened by the requirements of digital living. This awareness can also complement the trend towards minimalism.

Digital decluttering also allows you to prepare your digital legacy. Long after you've passed away, your information will still be available. It's not easy to think about our own mortality but it has become an essential part of estate planning. While alive, you get to decide what information you leave behind and who will have access to it after you're gone. If you don't make arrangements in advance, some data may become inaccessible and other data might be used in undesirable ways.

As you can see, the time invested in digital decluttering has many benefits. I consider myself an advocate for living an integrated digital life that includes both digital and analog components. An integrated digital life includes the mindful use of technology to achieve your goals. You choose what devices you have and how you use them. And, whenever possible, use the power you have to decide what data you create and what data you keep.

12.3 **Free Yourself from Unwanted Files**

1. *Start with the easy stuff:* Go through your computer's files. Discard the ones you don't want or need. Then empty the trash can or recycle bin so you can't go back and retrieve them later. Use the rule of 12. If you haven't used the file for 12 or more months, you probably don't need it. If it is an important file, like a bill, medical

information, or tax forms, put it in a folder labeled "Important Documents" and leave it on your computer where you can access the files at any time.

2. *Manage Your Media:* File your music, photos, and other media in the appropriate folders. Make them easy to find by keeping them on your desktop where they can be easily seen. You can keep your desktop clutter free by making a master media folder and then creating sub folders for the different media formats. Just like with your files, go through and delete any media you don't want or need to keep anymore. Deleting the unwanted files will free up space on your hard drive and give

you the ability to download other media in the future.

3. *Pick Your Programs:* Did you download Picasso thinking you were going to edit all your vacation pictures, but then forgot to do it? Uninstall the programs you don't use anymore. This will help speed up your computer and reduce the risk of you having potentially malware targeted software taking up space on your hard drive.

4. *Strengthen and Store Your Passwords:* Review all your passwords. Strengthen and change them as you see fit. Make sure all your passwords are unique and use letters (Upper and

Lower Case) and numbers. If you have a lot of passwords to remember download and use a password manager. Password managers help you by remembering all your passwords so that you don't have to.

5. *Back That Data Up:* Ideally, you are backing up your important data all the time. However, if you haven't done it in a while...or ever, consider doing it now. Use a portable hard drive or cloud service to make sure that your files exist in a place outside of your home or office. This will ensure that if anything happens to your computer like it crashes or

implodes, you won't lose all your data.

6. *Reinstall Your Operating System:* Once you have successfully backed up all your data you might consider reinstalling your operating system. While it may not seem necessary with modern technology, it is always nice to start fresh. Reinstalling has the potential to speed up your computer. Not sure how to reinstall? Just do a google search for "How to reinstall Windows/MAC (insert version here)."

7. *Set-Up Internet Security:* You should get an antivirus, anti-phishing and anti-spyware

software as well as a firewall. If you already have them simply perform updates to make sure they are running at their optimum level. If you don't, do your research and choose software the will best meet your needs. If you want to add an extra layer of security you can get a VPN (Virtual Private Network) for the time you use free Wi-Fi. Try ProXPN for free and see what all the VPN hype is about.

8. *Refresh Your Phone:* Go through all your devices and perform system updates. Then review and delete any unwanted apps to free up space. Use that free space to download a security app for your phone. These apps can help

ensure that no one is hacking into your phone's data. Both iPhone and Android users can try Lookout for free in the app store or on Google Play.

Do these 8 tasks and eliminate the digital clutter from your life. Making it a priority to organize your digital life will help give you peace of mind. So in-between dusting the ceiling fans and shampooing the carpets, take a few minutes to clean up your digital clutter. Trust us, you will be glad you did!

Your Quick Start Action Step: Start by making it searchable

Digital clutter doesn't always need to be "organized," and it mostly doesn't need frequent cleaning, with the possible exception of if someone else is going to be sharing it. It does need to be searchable, however, so you can find what you want when you want it and that you know what you have for when you are ultimately ready to get rid of the junk. Judicious use of tags, titles, and keywords can help.

Conclusion

Thank you again for owning this book!

I hope it was able to help you to achieve your personal mental decluttering goals, whatever it is that they may be. Just because you've finished this book doesn't mean there is nothing left to learn on the topic, and expanding your horizons is the only way to find the mastery you seek. The next step is to stop reading already and to get ready to get started cleaning the mental clutter from your mind once and for all.

While you are no doubt anxious to get started, it is important to do so with realistic expectations in mind, especially if you feel as though you have been hanging on to mental clutter for quite some time. While the human brain is certainly capable of developing new ways of looking at the world, these sorts of things take time. In fact, depending on the amount of clutter you are dealing with, it could take weeks or even months of hard work before you start seeing results. It is important to not lose faith in the interim, however, as you will only find the success you seek if you keep up the good work. As such, it is best to think of decluttering your mind as a marathon, not a sprint, which means that slow and steady wins the race.

Thank you and good luck!

Preview Of 'Minimalist Budget' by Marie S. Davenport

Chapter 6 – Dealing with Debt

6.1

The simplest way to describe debt is money that is owed from one party to the other. It may get complicated quickly. It all depends on the amount of debt you have and the way you handle it. Debt can be a useful tool or baggage that complicates your life.

Knowing the right way to handle debt can be difficult especially if you constantly struggle to cover your monthly bills. There are various ways to handle each type of debt. There are also ways to get relief from debt. Just be careful of companies that sound too good to be true or promise you absurd things. Here are the two most common types of debt and ways to handle them:

- **Secured debt**: A secured debt is one where the borrower has provided some asset as collateral to secure the loan. Mortgages and car loans are examples of a secured debt. If you don't pay, the creditor can take the said asset like foreclosing your house or repossessing your car.

- **Unsecured debt** is never backed by an asset. One example is a credit card. This doesn't mean you won't have consequences if you don't pay your bills. The creditor can sell your debt to a collection agency that will then call you night and day for payment. If you still don't pay, they might be able to sue you

for payment. This might lead to
your wages being garnished.
Some creditors might sue you
without using a collection agency.

6.2

Most people wonder how much of their
money is theirs and the amount they pay
toward debt factors in on how their debt
is accumulated. There are many reasons
why we have debt, such as
unemployment or unforeseen
emergencies. More often than not, debt
is caused by bad spending habits. If you
aren't paying with cash, it will cost you
to spend money.

Think about a credit card being

somebody who is granting you a favor to buy things you cannot afford but will let you pay them off later. Actually, the truth is you just wind up owing more and not getting everything you need.

Everybody alive tries to keep up with their neighbors. They have the life we've always wished for, and we will never be able to keep up with them. These things we long for lead us to huge amounts of debt. When we don't know how to manage this debt, it can cause our credit card bills to grow endlessly.

Let's look at making a purchase of $500 without a credit card. You think this is a good deal because you only have to pay $15 a month. This is very manageable for you. What you don't realize is the creditor is adding an additional $147 to that bill for interest. If you only pay $15 each month, it is going to take you four years to pay off that $500 charge. That is assuming you have an interest rate of 14.7 percent. If your credit card has a higher interest rate, this purchase at 22 percent means you are going to be paying out an additional $280 in interest. Yes, you still have those four years to pay off a total of $780, so is that item worth that much more?

If you add in all our wants with the large investments of cars and homes along with the planned necessities like weddings and college as well as the unplanned emergencies like relocation, unemployment, and medical emergencies, it is easy to visualize how quickly debt can grow. The main reason people get into debt is a combination of personal and impersonal finances.

6.3

Even if your debt is small, you have to manage it well. You have to make your payments on time and be sure it doesn't get out of hand. If your debt is large, you must put in more effort to pay it off while making your other payments.

1. *Know your creditors and the amounts you owe.*

Create a list of debts that include

the creditor, complete amount you owe, how much your payments are, and when they are due. Use a credit report to confirm your debts. Having the debts in front of you lets you see the bigger picture, so you are aware of your whole debt. Don't make a list and then forget about it. Look at it from time to time, especially when you pay your bills. Update the list every month or two when the list changes.

2. *Pay your dues on time.*

Making late payments will make it harder for you to pay off the debt because you are going to have to pay an extra late fee for each payment you miss. If you miss two payments, your finance charges and interest rate will go up. If you use a calendar, place your payments and set an alarm to give you an alert a couple days before the payment needs to be made. If you miss a payment, don't wait until it becomes due again. The creditor may report it to a credit bureau. Make your payment once you remember.

3. Make a bill-paying calendar.

Use a calendar to help you figure out what bill to pay with a certain paycheck. Write every bill's payment on the day it is due. Next, put in the calendar when you get paid. If you get paid on the same date, this is an easy step for you. If your paychecks come on a different day, it will help to make a note each month.

4. ***Always make your minimum payment.***

If the minimum amount is all you can pay, that is fine—just do it on time. This isn't going to get you any progress in paying off your debt. It will keep the debt from growing and will keep your account good. If you miss a payment, it becomes harder to get caught up. Your account may go into default.

5. *Figure out what debt you need to pay off fastest.*

Paying off any credit card debt first is the best strategy since these have higher interest rates. It must be the priority since it will cost you the most money. Use your list of debts, and rank them in order that you want to pay them off. You may also choose to pay off the one with the lowest balance first.

6. *Pay off any charge-offs and*

collections.

You can only pay what you can afford. If you have limited funds to repay debts, try to focus on keeping other accounts in good standing. Never sacrifice good accounts for ones that have already changed your credit. Pay the past due accounts when you can afford them. These creditors are going to keep hounding you for payment until it is brought current.

7. *Have an emergency fund to help out in hard situations.*

You may have to go into debt to

cover an emergency if you don't want to dip into your savings account. A small emergency fund can cover small expenses that may pop up now and then. Begin by working to create a small fund. An amount of $ 1,000 is a great place to start. When you have that amount, try to increase it to another thousand. You want to try to create a reserve that equals your six months' pay.

8. *Create a monthly budget to plan expenses.*

Keeping a budget will help you make sure that you have the money to cover all expenses each month. Plan in advance so that you can take action if you are going to be short one month. Budgets help you plan how to use any extra money you may have left after all expenses have been paid. You may have enough money to pay another debt off.

9. See the signs that you are in need of help.

If you see that it is too hard for you to pay your bills and debts every month, you can turn to a debt relief company for help. Check out credit counseling agencies in your area. Other options are bankruptcy, debt

settlement, and debt
consolidation. All of these have
disadvantages and advantages, so
check each option carefully. If
you have a spending problem,
you can seek help through a
Debtors Anonymous group. This
is similar to Alcoholics
Anonymous.

10. *Change Your Debt Like Behaviors*

In order to get out of debt, you
have to eliminate the reasons you
may up in debt in the first place.
Even winning the Powerball
Jackpot won't fix your problem if
you don't learn how to spend less

than what you make.

Everybody has their own reasons for winding up in debt. Medical bills, job loss, school, or just plain young stupidity are all widely common reasons. However, the reason you have gotten into debt doesn't matter all that much. What matters the most is that you don't let this happen again. Here are some things you must not do:

- If you have to take out $50k in student loans to get your bachelor's degree, don't take out an extra $100k for a Ph.D.

- Did you end up falling into a large pile of debt when you lost your job? Resolve, after you have gotten out of debt, to work on building up an emergency fund so that you won't have to face this problem again.

- If you spend several years living a life that you can't afford, then you have to figure out the life that you can actually afford, and get to that point.

That last point is a lot easier said than done. The truth is that the last point is the main reason for this book and about a third of all financial articles you can find online. Let's be honest: how many articles have you seen that are labeled, "Live within your means," "Spend less than your monthly income," and so on? Why has there been so much stuff written on this very simple concept?

This is because after a person has gotten used to living in a certain way, it is extremely hard to change that habit. It will be like having to live on ramen after living for two years on The Capital Grille.

11. When to Refinance or

Consolidate

Two of the most common things people do when faced with a lot of debt is consolidation and refinancing. Consolidation means that you put all of your debts into one loan. This will help you by allowing you to deal with only one lender. This means you won't be faced with several different monthly billing statements.

Refinancing means that you replace all of your old debts with a new loan. The goal of doing this is to get a lower interest rate. The majority of students will use consolidation for their student loans. This works if all of the debts are from a government program.

There are many different online calculators to help you figure out if refinancing works for you and to make sure that you pick the best one. Before you decide to consolidate or refinance, take the following into consideration:

- Has your credit score gone up any? This will place you in a favorable light with lenders. This means you will be able to start a tangible process of removing all of your old debt with a new lender that offer better terms.

- Do you already have low-interest rates? If this is the case, you can take advantage of it. Change your variable rate to a fixed rate.

- Are you able to change your payment terms? Dragging your debt along with you for a long time won't help you to become debt-free. If you are making more money and can afford it, start making larger payments each month.

Your Quick Start Action Step:

You are not alone in your debt. Most people in the world are also in debt. If you live in denial, it will only increase your money problems along with your anxiety. When you can face your situation, paying off those debts may be easier than you realize.

- Fast facts: The first thing you have to do is to figure out how big your problem is. Start by looking at your last bank statement and finding any missing paperwork. Open bills you have been neglecting. Create a list of the amount you owe every company and their interest rates. When you have figured out this information, you will begin to prioritize all your debts.

- Transfer to a zero-percent credit card. If you have expensive credit cards, see if you can transfer the debt to a zero-percent credit card. These cards can eliminate interest charges for a certain period. This makes sure that every cent you repay will go toward paying down your balance. In order to get the most out of these cards, you need to pay off the balance in the offer window. If you know you can't repay the whole amount in the introductory period, look for low-interest rate cards. You are still going to pay interest every month, but it will be at a low rate. These types of cards require an unblemished credit score.

- Think about overdraft options. If you pay a lot of interest in overdraft fees, this can quickly accelerate your debt problems. If you think you may be paying too much for your overdraft service, see if your bank has a different account you can switch to, or drop the overdraft from your account entirely.

- You may consider a personal loan. There may be a time when getting a personal loan can help you manage your debt. Find a leading market rate with the APR lower than what you are currently paying on your credit card. If you look around, it may be possible to find a rate lower than eight percent. This is a lot better than the normal 17 to 22 percent that normal credit cards charge. If you need to borrow a large sum of money, a personal loan is a way to go. Larger loans usually come with lower APRs than those with smaller amounts. Don't borrow more money than you need since this may increase your chances of getting deeper into debt. Always shop around. You aren't going to get a good rate if you accept the first offer from the first lender you go to.

Chapter 7 –
Overall Budget
Techniques
Applied to Daily,
Monthly, and
Long-Term
Expenses

7.1

We've used the word budget and budgeting a lot throughout this book. While it may sound like a bad word to many, especially for those who know how taking a deeper look at their finances is going to reveal some pretty bad habits that they would rather stay hidden, it is an extremely helpful tool when it comes to a minimalist budget.

Budgeting is known to be difficult, even when it comes to just keeping track of where all of your money goes. The first question people will ask you is if you are trying to budget before taxes (i.e. gross income) or after taxes (i.e. net income)?

If you want to begin with your gross income, it will be best to look at the percentage that is saved in your 401(k). If your company offers you a match offer, make sure you put away enough to get it. The maximum contribution of an employee for a 401(k) is $18,000 in 2016, so try not to go over this limit. However, this does not include what your employer will contribute. The limit for you and your employer's contribution is $53,000. You can also have health insurance premiums that are automatically deducted from your pay if your company provides you insurance, so there is a chance that you won't have to include this into your post-tax budget.

After you have become comfortable with

how your payroll and pre-tax deduction saving works, you can then focus on your budget for net income, which is what most people look at day-to-day. If you plan on being really minimalist with your budget, here is a suggestion: the 65-25-10 rule.

- 65% is spent on your day-to-day living.
- 25% is spent on large expenses and retirement, including emergencies.
- 10% is given away to your favorite causes or charity.

You can get really nitty-gritty about it, and break them down even further. However, when you are trying to see the big picture, sometimes it's good just to have a few numbers. If you have to provide your own savings, then you may want the breakdown to be 65-15-10-10.

- 65% is still day-to-day expenses.
- 15% is your emergency and large expenses.
- 10% is retirement expenses.
- 10% is charity expenses.

The hard decisions are made in the day-to-day expenses. If you make sure that you automate your savings money and set them aside, you will make sure that you won't spend the amount that you intended to save on eating out or impulse buys because the money won't be in your checking account.

When you are first starting out with budgeting, or when you are trying to get a handle on your spending, try using a cash-only method or limit yourself a lot when it comes to using your credit card. If you do use a credit card, start going in and manually categorizing and entering your purchases so that you will become aware of the things you are spending.

Much like how you log your calories when you want to lose weight, typing in each dollar you spend into a spreadsheet will help you to become more aware of the way you use your money, which is the first step you need to take toward financial success.

After you have gotten a handle on your spending, you can upgrade to a program that will download your credit card and bank information so that you won't have to write everything down by hand, but make sure that you still set aside some time to really look over your weekly spending so that you can see how you are balancing yourself across different categories. If you overspend in one category, that's okay—just try to under-spend in another one.

This budgeting will require a bit of work on your part—but in the end, it will help you save for and spend on the things that are the most important.